DIARY OF A CRICKET LOVER

Around the Counties

with

Vernon Coleman

This book is copyright. Enquiries should be addressed to the author.
Copyright© Vernon Coleman
The right of Vernon Coleman to be identified as the author of this work has been asserted in accordance with the Copyright, Designs and Patents Act 1988.

A catalogue record for this book is available from the British Library.

The author Vernon Coleman MB ChB DSc is a registered medical practitioner. He is the author of over 100 other books, many of which are available as Kindle books on Amazon. For a list of books please see Vernon Coleman's author page on Amazon or visit *http://www.vernoncoleman.com/*

To Sue.
And to Albert Norman Other,
A cricket lover of incomparable worth.

Sunday 1st January
I know that some people would argue that the beginning of January heralds the real beginning of winter. But for me the first day of the new calendar marks a point right in the middle of the winter, between the end of one cricket season and the start of another.

Like most enthusiastic cricket lovers, I manage to keep going through the months from mid-September to late April on an occasional and far from satisfying diet of crackly radio reports and taste-teasing newspaper columns. I often think that the one real joy of being outrageously rich would be in being able to fly off to Australia or the West Indies to watch a few days cricket. I am sure I remember reading that Mick Jagger had once flown off on a whim to watch a couple of days cricket. Now that is a really sound way to use money.

Thursday 5th January
Spent the evening looking through last season's scorecards. I have not thrown away a score card for several years now and I am beginning to amass quite a collection. I quite wish I had always kept my score cards — they make a useful and pleasant adjunct to *Wisden*. I do not know whether my memory is beginning to go but I sometimes have tremendous difficulty in remembering just which matches I have seen. Looking at last year's cards they bring back some wonderful memories. The first match I saw was apparently at the Parks at the end of April where I watched the University playing Lancashire, who were trying out one or two newcomers.

It was chilly and fairly dark and I am reminded that I saw my first 'bad light' decision of the year within thirty-minutes of arriving on the ground.

Monday 9th January
I did very well in the sales today. I bought a bright yellow anorak with a detachable hood, two huge travelling rugs, a charcoal fired hand-warmer, a new vacuum flask, a massive golfing umbrella and a pair of waterproof trousers. These should all help to see me through the season.

Thursday 10th January
Today, in wildly extravagant mood, I bought a solid silver hip flask. It will hold a fifth of a bottle of whisky. Added to the items I bought yesterday it helps make up an excellent cricket-watching kit.

Saturday 28th January
When visiting London during the winter I often take advantage of my MCC membership and leave my car parked at Lords. I do not do this just because the car parking is free (by the time I have taken a cab to my destination and then taken one back again to pick up the car it is probably more expensive than parking in one of the underground or multi-storey car parks in central London) but because I rather like to call in and take a quick look found. It is remarkably soothing in the middle of winter to know that within a few weeks cricketers will be out there on the square and the ground will once again be packed with enthusiastic spectators.

Today, I had a few minutes to spare, so, in addition to taking a quick walk round the ground, I decided to take a look inside the pavilion; just to make sure that nothing had changed. When I wandered into the Long Room I was approached by a pleasant, rather elderly gentleman in a pair of grey flannels and a sports jacket.

'Wonderful isn't it?' he said, as I stared longingly out of the windows onto the remarkably green looking turf.

I nodded in silent agreement.

The gentleman in the flannels and sports coat obviously took my silence as some sort of signal; he clearly mistook me for a tourist who had wandered into the Long Room by mistake. With tremendous enthusiasm and an unstoppable flow of history he proceeded to treat me to a thirty-minute lecture on the history of Lords, the game itself, the rooms in the pavilion and the members of the Marylebone Cricket Club.

I listened with as much politeness as I could muster and finally took my leave; claiming that I had to rush to get to see Tower Bridge before it closed.

Next time I call in at Lords in winter I will make sure I am wearing my MCC tie.

Sunday 5th February
Spent the morning oiling my binoculars. Last year they stuck several times and I am quite determined that I shall not have the same problem this year. There seems to be a spare lens fitted into them because I have one left over. I think this is a rather impressive gesture on the part of the manufacturers.

Thursday 9th February
I heard at dinner today about the huge television screen that they have at Melbourne Cricket Ground. The screen is used to show action replays to spectators and apparently the response has been very mixed. On the

one hand, there are those who welcome the innovation since it enable spectators to savour fine shots, good catches and skilful fielding. I must confess that I sympathise with this attitude. Like many other cricket lovers I have become so used to watching replays on television that when I am watching a live match I often feel frustrated by not being able to see a replay of the most exciting events. (And since those most exciting moments invariably seem to take place while I am buying food or drink the replay would probably be the *only* chance I got to see *some* of the better moments.)

On the other hand, I rather abhor this introduction of high technology into what is, after all, a game made quite complicated enough by its own rules and regulations. Where will the technology stop? Will the umpires be given small screens to hold in their pockets? Or will monitors be built into the wickets? And what happens if the action replay screen breaks down? Does play have to be held up while the TV repairman is called in? And, perhaps most important of all, who on earth wants to be an umpire under those circumstances? Even the most confident of men would be bound to flinch a little at the prospect of seeing his decisions examined in close-up detail, and at slow-motion leisure.

At the moment they do not show controversial decisions on their big screen at Melbourne. But who decides what is controversial, and will all grounds be as conscientious?

Thursday 16th February
I wonder why it is that so few Australians play in English county cricket? There are New Zealanders, West Indians, Indians, Pakistanis and South Africans galore. But remarkably few Australian players,

although I have heard rumours that Terry Alderman is due to spend the season over here with Kent.

If our domestic game is to be dominated by overseas players it would be pleasant to see one or two more Australians around. They sometimes seem an uncouth bunch, but they do take their cricket very seriously and I cannot help feeling that some of our younger players would benefit from playing alongside such determined professionals.

Thursday 8th March
So many internationally famous cricketers from the West Indies, England and Sri Lanka have now been banned from their national sides for playing in South African that I cannot help wondering how long it will be before a tournament for banned players is arranged.

I am surprised that the South Africans have not thought of it already. I cannot believe it would be difficult to find sponsors for a limited-over tournament between West Indians, English players, South Africans and players from Sri Lanka. They could call it the Alternative World Cup and invite Mrs Gandhi to present the medals.

(I wonder why there are no banned Australian players around — and why the Australians have been reluctant to play cricket in South Africa? Many white Australians treat aborigines as though they were inferior beings; I cannot believe that the Australian people as a whole find contact with South Africa particularly abhorrent.)

Friday 23rd March
Last year I got fed up with fishing flies out of my lager at cricket matches. I tried to get into the habit of putting a paperback book on the top of the glass in order to

keep the flies out, though I usually forgot. I decided that the only sensible solution would be to buy one of those mugs with lids on that the Germans are so fond of However, although I must have tried just about every shop in the country I just could not find a lidded drinking mug. And then today, up in Newcastle, I saw exactly what I wanted in the window of a shop selling pewter. It cost rather more than I had expected, but it will surely pay for itself in a few months if you consider the amount of lager that I had to throw away last year.

Saturday 6th April
Looking at the details of last winter's Currie Cup in South Africa I cannot help wondering whether I will ever see the like of Barrie Richards again. It would have been marvellous to see him play against the great fast bowlers of his era. He must have felt cheated at being denied a chance against Lillee, Thomson, Holding and Roberts at international level. I certainly felt cheated as a spectator.

    I wonder how long we are going to allow the politicians to interfere so cruelly with cricket? I cannot think of any other sport which is so badly affected.

    The South African Grand Prix takes place this weekend. Cars and drivers from all over the world will take part in the race without anyone batting an eyelid. No one will suggest that the drivers approve of apartheid just because they race motor cars there.

Thursday 12th April
Today I met an Australian publisher who has flown over to meet a few British authors. He insisted on talking about the debacle of last winter's tour of Australia but I protested that I did not know why he

was so pleased. I told him that the England team that had been so roundly thrashed by the Australians had been an unofficial team put together by a group of cricketing dissidents and that the matches that had been played had been worthless in historical terms. I insisted that the Ashes had not been at stake and that none of the players who had toured Australia would ever have got into a proper England side.

He seemed confused.

Saturday 21st April

Norman Gifford had a tremendous season for Warwickshire last year; there must have been a few red faces down at Worcester. I bet they wished they had kept him there. Now I gather that Ormrod is leaving the county too — this time to go to Lancashire.

Both these players have served Worcester well for many years. It seems a pity that they cannot finish their careers with the county.

But there have been many instances over the years of cricketers leaving a county side in their thirties or early forties and having new and successful careers with different sides. One wonders if they would have had similar success if they had stayed with their old teams? There must be great stimulation in starting a new career with a new county.

Sunday 22nd April

Bats have been oiled, pads and boots whitened, chunky white sweaters shaken free of mothballs, sandwich fingers flexed, grounds rolled and mown, pitches cut and marked, fixture lists printed and distributed, boundary ropes uncoiled, membership and car park passes mailed and received with welcome smiles, creaky joints exercised in the nets, catching cradle repaired and put into action; umpires have collected their coats from the dry cleaners and their pebbles from the bedroom drawer, secretaries have sent off cheques for. new cricket balls, groundsmen have hunted high and low for missing bails, wives have resigned themselves to lonely weekends, girlfriends have made promises that some will regret as the summer continues, sponsors and advertisers have wooed the famous and been wooed by the impecunious, ambitions have been reawakened and retirements postponed. The preparations are complete. Another cricket season is about to start.

Tuesday 24th April
The season does not really start until tomorrow when the MCC meet Essex at Lords. But as part of their pre-season practice, Warwickshire invariably play their local rivals, Worcestershire, in a friendly one-day match. So today I collected together my cricket watching kit (pencils, notebooks, binoculars, vacuum flask, sandwich box, anorak, silver hip flask, German-style drinking mug, waterproof trousers, umbrella etc) and set off for Edgbaston.

It was marvellous to see the ground again after the long winter and wonderful to see so many familiar faces. Over the years I have got on nodding terms, and occasional speaking terms, with quite a number of other cricket lovers. On the whole, I do not know their names nor what they do for a living; for me, I admit, they have no life outside the cricket grounds where I am accustomed to seeing them. But they are dear friends nevertheless and it is always good to see that the English winter has not affected their number. I remember that at the start of last season there was one particular old fellow missing. He had always been a faithful follower of Warwickshire and when by mid-May he still had not appeared on the ground I feared the worst. I was convinced that he had died, for I knew that it would need to be something pretty serious to keep him away from his beloved cricket. I knew neither his name nor his address, however, so there was no way that I could find out what had happened to him.

And then, right at end of May, he reappeared. I was so pleased to see him that I broke with tradition, spoke to him and insisted on buying him a cup of tea. It turned out that he had fallen on an icy pavement and broken his hip. They had told him in hospital that he would need to stay in bed until August and that he would be lucky to leave the hospital at all. But cricket watchers are made of sterner stuff than ordinary folks. He was not prepared to let a mere trifle like a broken hip interfere with more than a month or so of his cricket watching.

It was, I must confess, the renewal of interrupted friendships that made that day for me There was Eddie, for example, alongside whom I have shared the joy of a few spectacular wins, and the sorrow of too many uncomfortable defeats. Eddie works a steward for British Airways and during the winter plays for an airline team that organises matches in such locations as the Bahamas. I had received a series of tantalising postcards from him during the bleak, dark months of the winter, but I had not seen him since September. And there, too, was Henry, who works as a foreman at a large car factory, but who also bowls quicker than his physical form might suggest for a Birmingham league side. I should think that it is comparatively easy to keep factory discipline when you are known as the Erdington Demon.

It was good, too, to see familiar faces serving behind the sandwich bar and to see that in a year when everyone else seems to be eating bran cereals, natural yoghurt and hunks of raw pineapple, cricket spectators are expected to continue their normal diet of pork pies, scotch eggs, sausage rolls, cornish pasties and beef sandwiches.

While selecting a suitably unhealthy mixture from the available collection I found myself queueing beside John Inchmore, the Worcestershire fast bowler. The unfortunate Inchmore was nursing a strained back and was unable to play. He told me that he has high hopes of being given a benefit with Worcestershire next year. A benefit season makes a huge difference to a player's life. Inevitably, he is on tenterhooks to know what the committee had decided.

Talking both to Inchmore and to other players over the last few years, I have become more and more confused about just how various counties decide which players are to have benefits — and when. It does not seem as though there are any hard and fast rules about it. Play for one county and you will automatically get a benefit after ten years as a capped player. Play for another county and you can expect a benefit long before you have been playing for that long. Nor is there any way to tell how much money will be raised. If you play for one of the larger, better organised counties, you can hope to raise a hundred thousand pounds by the end of your allotted season. If you play your professional cricket for a smaller county then a ten thousand pound benefit will be a good one.

Of course, benefits have all become exceptionally well-organised these days. A few years ago most cricketers relied very heavily on the take from their allotted match and expected to add a collection and perhaps a raffle or two to this sum. Today the allotted matches are just one small part of the benefit; a cricketer will have dances, brochures, dinners, raffles and all sorts of other fund raising schemes. Organising a benefit can be so complex and so costly that I have even heard of one cricketer who made a *loss* on his benefit year. He spent more on organising his benefit than he collected, and if is rumoured that, tragically, he had to sell his house to pay the debts.

When a cricketer does do well, however, the money he makes is made much more valuable by the fact that he does not have to pay income tax on it. Many are now becoming worried by the fact that well-known cricketers (who probably need the money rather less than cricketers who have not achieved Test status) seem determined to raise huge six-figure sums. It seems likely that if this happens too often then the tax collector will start demanding a share. The ordinary county player will then find his benefit less worthwhile.

Meanwhile, John Inchmore is worrying, not about the tax problems he may or may not have, but about whether or not he is going to get a benefit next year. Believe it or not, benefits these days need so much planning that if Inchmore does not find out soon he will not be able to take full advantage of the opportunity.

Monday 23rd April
I have sharpened several pencils and managed to scrape all the mustard off my rubber. I have also cleaned out the thermos flask which I found, to my shame, still contained half a cupful of cold, black coffee from the final fixture at Worcester last year. For several years now I have carried my impediments to cricket matches in a fishing bag, I find I need something fairly spacious

to cram in books, notebooks, pencils, sandwiches, flask, apples, anorak, and all the other equipment essential to good cricket watching. However, I do not think that the fishing bag is going to be big enough now that I have got a new hip flask and a pewter mug with a lid to take around with me. Now I know why so many people like to watch cricket while sitting in their cars. They just cannot carry all the stuff they have brought with them.

Wednesday 25th April
The first real cricket watching day of the season. Lords was quite busy and the weather was splendid. It was Sue's first day at the game's physical and spiritual headquarters and she was quite indignant when she found out that women are not allowed in the pavilion. She suggested lightheartedly that before long the feminists will put a stop to this little bit of parochial chauvinism. I told her that one of the few things I am sure of in this world is that the Lords pavilion will remain a male preserve for at least another century or two; I pointed out that whatever new laws might be passed to outlaw such social discrimination the members would always be able to keep ahead of the legislators. When she demurred I pointed out that in a crisis it would be possible to put urinals in the Long Room. This would effectively turn the whole of the pavilion into a gentleman's convenience.

   The cricket was well worth watching today. It was. splendid to see young Andy Lloyd of Warwickshire getting a chance to prove himself and I strongly suspect that before the season is over we will see him in an England Sweater. It was also marvellous to see Graham Gooch in action — even if Mrs Gandhi and her pals still will not let him play for England. The day was kept from getting too exciting by the dullness of Chris Smith, who makes dear old Boycott look positively exciting. After today's performance I cannot see; Smith getting any more England caps unless timeless Tests are brought back in.

Tuesday 26th April
This is the second day of the season's opening match and my very good friend Russell Smith came along to share the sunshine and entertainment. It was absolutely boiling hot and more like June than April. To take advantage of the glorious weather we sat at the Nursery End. Russ had brought a martini-making kit which consisted of a bottle of gin, a half-empty bottle of vermouth, a bottle of olives and three long stemmed glasses. While Russ poured, Sue slipped out of the ground to the shops near the tube station. When she returned a few minutes later she was clutching a huge paper bag which turned out to contain a splendid liver pâté, a long French loaf a tin of caviar and a packet of thin toast-like biscuits.

Cricket watching can sometimes be very civilised. I had intended to start work on a book I am supposed to be writing, but somehow the day went by without my putting a word down in the notebook I had by my side.

Friday 27th April
A friend of mine called Malcolm Mortimer, who works for Radio Trent, the local commercial radio station in Nottingham, tells me that he is playing cricket on Sunday for his local team, Lenton United. He seems unsure about the opponents but claims that his slow left-arm deliveries are something quite remarkable. He insists that I turn up to watch, promising an

entertaining afternoon while he dazzles the opposition with his unreadable and unplayable deliveries.

Saturday 28th April
My binoculars seem to have stopped working. I had a lot of trouble with them but I did think that it was perhaps a side effect from Russ's martini-making kit. When I first discovered the fault I thought I had gone blind in one eye. It was a considerable relief to discover that the fault lay with the glasses and not with my eyes. I am not at all sure what has gone wrong but it is rather surprising since I see from my diary that I took them apart earlier this year (5th February) and gave them a good cleaning.

Sunday 29th April
Turned up to watch young Mortimer playing for Lenton United. The team's ground is hidden away on the outskirts of the city and we spent several hours wandering around looking for the match. It is remarkable just how many cricket matches take place on Sundays in the Nottingham area. Bat, pad and ball manufacturers should concentrate their sales efforts on this part of the country. By the time we found the right ground I had watched bits and pieces of seven other matches.

Unfortunately, by the time we got there, Mortimer's side had batted and I had missed my friend's skills with the bat. But his side was about to take the field and so I settled down to watch the proceedings with some interest.

I felt cheated when the match ended and Mortimer still had not bowled a ball. He insisted afterwards that it was became he had a row with the captain. We discussed captaincy at some length in the pub later and agreed that it is quite invidious that one man should have such absolute authority. We had planned a picnic supper but it was bitterly cold in Nottingham (in much contrast to the weather at Lords a few days ago). Although it is still only April I felt rather cross about this, as though some generous and unexpected gift had been snatched away.

Saturday 5th May
At Trent Bridge today I met a good friend of mine whom I have not seen for years. He is now working as a general practitioner just down the road in Leicestershire and although he is a member at Grace Road he prefers the atmosphere at Trent Bridge. I do not think this is meant as any sort of a slight on the Leicester club but is rather a tribute to my friend's past. He studied medicine in Nottingham and spent a good deal of his six years in the city watching cricket rather than tending to patients. Going to Trent Bridge for the day reminds him of his days at medical school.

My friend, whom I will call Dr H, for the very good reason that neither his first name nor his surname begin with the letter H, had brought with him a large picnic hamper. It was one of those old-fashioned wicker hampers and it seemed to contain just about every delicacy known to man. There were four different kinds of pâté, three different types of cheese (including an excellent Stilton and a very fine Brie), a loaf of French bread, an excellent mixed salad, a large plastic container filled with strawberries and another filled with cream and a whole host of other titbits designed to titillate the palate and satisfy the stomach. In addition to the food, there was also an excellent bottle of claret, a bottle of dry white, and a bottle of champagne to go with the strawberries.

I did not take much persuading to share this feast.

I cannot remember exactly when we started our lunch but I suppose that it must have been somewhere around noon. And if it is difficult to say just when we started, it is even more difficult to say when we finished. All I can say with any certainty is that we finished the last of the strawberries and the last of the champagne just as the official luncheon interval came to an end.

It was at that point that my friend produced a large flask of black coffee. I thought that this was an excellent idea and I told him so with great enthusiasm. I am not all that good at coping with wine for lunch and three bottles shared with just one person is more than enough to damage my faculties and send me off to sleep.

The afternoon was quite extraordinary. I honestly cannot remember anything about the cricket. Without looking up the fixture in the calendar I cannot even tell you who was playing whom or what the competition was. And I never did find my scorecard although I am sure it must be somewhere. By half past two I knew that I had drunk far too much; I was determined to sober myself up for the evening. Oddly enough, however, by three I felt worse than I had at two. I decided that the wine was having a delayed effect and I drank another large cup of black coffee. By four I felt worse than I had at three. And I drank more coffee.

By half past five there was absolutely no coffee left in the flask and I remember feeling a good deal worse than I had at four.

With some slurring I congratulated my friend on the state of his liver. He had drunk hardly any black coffee at all but seemed far less inebriated than I. I commented on this extraordinary feet as an example of the way that one body will cope with insults far more effectively than another.

My friend seemed slightly confused.

So I explained yet again that I was impressed that he had managed to stay sober without drinking heaps of black coffee.

It took my friend the best part of ten minutes to stop the tears pouring down his cheeks and to halt the hysterical laughter that threatened to tear his body in half.

When he did finally manage to stop himself laughing long enough to talk he explained that what I had thought had been plain black coffee had been Russian coffee, strongly laced with vodka. While I thought I was sobering myself up I was busy getting absolutely plastered. I left my car at the ground, my friend gave me a lift to the station, and I finally got home by train and taxi.

Sunday 13th May

For the first time this season I settled down this afternoon to watch one of the John Player Special League one-day matches on television. I am not quite sure why, but the standard of television commentary always seems to me to fail to match up to the standard of radio commentary. During Test Matches, like so many people I know, I turn down the sound on the television set and listen to the radio commentators. Today there was no such alternative and so I had to sit and listen to a lot of inane and unnecessary wittering. The odd thing is that the same people work on both the radio and the television. It is, perhaps, the chummy atmosphere in the Radio Three commentary box that gives that medium the edge. The radio commentary seems to follow the relaxed, comfortable and friendly style of the inimitable Brian Johnston. The television commentary seems to owe too much to the humourless Richie Benaud, whose taste in ties and jackets betrays him as an intruder. (Why, I wonder, do Australians have such appalling dress sense?) After listening to Christopher Martin-Jenkins for half hour I tried turning down the sound completely. That did not work, however, because, without the click of ball on bat and the background hum of the crowd, the effect was rather spoilt.

The match was between Somerset and Hampshire and should have been exciting. But somehow it palled and I lost all interest. Is it just the commentators or has televised one-day cricket finally had its day? This match seemed meaningless and joyless.

While wondering why the afternoon's match was about as attractive as three hours of women's athletics between East Germany and Czechoslovakia, it occurred to me that those who offer us our television cricket might like to experiment a little with some of the magnificent new technology that they have available.

Surely it would be possible to use the sort of computerised control available through the Ceefax and Oracle systems to give viewers the chance to select for themselves the picture they received. So, for example, one could press one number to get an overall shot of the ground, another to get a shot from behind the bowler's arm and a third to obtain a close up of the batsman. With the use of six buttons one could pick and choose between the shorts provided by six different cameras - much in the same sort of way that a television director decides which picture to transmit. One could press additional buttons to obtain an up-to-date scorecard, bowling figures and so on. With this sort of facility, and an outside microphone recording the ground 'atmosphere', it would be perfectly possible to do away with commentators completely.

Tuesday 15th May
The only snag with writing books for a living is that when they are published you have to promote them. There are so many books coming out these days that it is no good expecting people to find a new book just because it's there on the shelves. The author has to go out on the road and actively promote his latest product. My latest book is no exception and I had a radio interview arranged for this afternoon. The morning, however, was free and there was a match between Middlesex and Sussex at Lords to look forward to.

Staying in London overnight you would think it would be easy to get to Lords in time to see the first ball bowled. We had a room at the National Liberal Club down in Whitehall, which, even at the busier times of day, cannot be more than half an hour away by car or black cab. Still, when time is not pressing, it is easy to end up being late. But I suppose it is more or less forgivable to be a little languid when you have spent two weeks tearing around intent on arriving at radio or television stations precisely on time.

As it was, we arrived just in time to see the West Indian touring team carrying their baggage over towards the nets for their first practice session. Even sauntering across to the Nursery End practice ground the West Indians looked fierce, threatening and professional. They have a loose, easy sort of confidence which they wear without any trace of arrogance. Some of their number, Clive Lloyd and Joel Gamer, for example, are instantly recognisable. Others, newer members of the squad, men who have yet to make their mark, may not have faces or names that mean much yet but they have already acquired that unique brand of jaunty confidence that helps to distinguish West Indian cricketers from all others. The Australians, at their very best and most successful have an arrant, crude, slightly overbearing confidence which is perhaps best described as cockiness. The Indians and Pakistanis, when they are playing well, have a quiet, smug sort of confidence which I find rather unpleasant. But the West Indians are good and they know that they are good and that is all there is to it. They enjoy being skilled and successful and there is nothing about them that could possibly give offence. They wear their great skill with simple, justifiable pride.

As we walked past the nets, watching while the West Indians unfastened cricket bags and tracksuit tops, Sue pointed to a tall, familiar, bespectacled figure circled by a clutch of small boys.

'Who's that?' she wanted to know.

I was slightly surprised that she had not recognised instantly one of the most famous cricketers in the world today, and explained that this was the great Clive Lloyd himself captain of the West Indian touring team, powerful, sometimes savage batsman and probably as fine a cover fielder as the game has ever known.

She had not heard of him.

I was shocked by this but these days it is, I suppose, quite common for someone to become extraordinarily famous in one particular field yet remain unknown to those not directly taking an interest in that sphere of activity. If you told me the names of the England soccer players, they would probably mean nothing at all to me. And yet these are men whose names appear in enormous block letters on the back pages of our newspapers throughout the winter;

I suspect that it requires something much more than skill or success to burst through the confining barriers of fame in a single sport or profession and become a 'household name', known even to those, who have no particular interest in your skills or capabilities. People like Muhammad Ali achieved great fame because his exploits took him out of the specialist pages and onto the general news pages. The archetypal cricket example is, I suppose, Ian Botham, whose clashes with the law and the authorities, as well as his at times phenomenal cricketing success, have gained him immense exposure.

These thoughts were still uppermost in my mind when I found that, almost unthinking, we had walked more or less right, round the ground and were now behind .the Tavern Bar. We bought two cornish pasties and two beakers of black coffee and wandered off into the almost deserted Mound Stand. There cannot have been more than a hundred spectators in the whole ground. It was, I daresay, the sort of turnout that most county secretaries would recognise as normal for a three county match.

We had been settled in our seats long enough to admire Daniel's fearsome pace and to wonder how many international sides could afford to leave a bowler of such threatening skills out of the reckoning when, with Sussex having scored just 32 for the loss of one wicket and the clock showing ten minutes to twelve, a man, coming from the Nursery End, walked .onto the pitch carrying a bucket of sawdust. It was as though this modest act of defiance was too much for the Gods. Before he had reached the bowlers run-up at the Pavilion End the drizzle started, and umpires and players alike set off for shelter. And that was that. The covers were brought on, the West Indian touring party entertained the Fleet Street, photographers by jogging around the ground and the rain teased and taunted for the rest of the day.

As an exercise in watching cricket it was less than successful. As a day of relaxation it was a tremendous success. There are few things more calming than sitting at a cricket ground where nothing is happening but where there is still promise of things to come. And the Lords caterers did us proud. The pasties tasted better and spicier than ever; we ate five between the two of us.

On the way to Nottingham that evening we passed, somewhere between Wellingborough and Leicester, a small village cricket ground. It was seven in the evening and so dark that it was difficult to see much although the players were well within hailing distance. It was drizzling lightly too and the tall, thick trees around the ground made it seem even darker. No cricketer paid to play the game would have contemplated cricket under such conditions. These players there for pleasure, were well set and clearly unlikely to be dissuaded by such inconsequential considerations as bad light or rain.

Saturday 19th May
My parents have a holiday flat on the seafront at Budleigh Salterton, down in Devon, and I arrived here two days ago to work on a newspaper article that needed finishing quickly. With the typescript safely completed, Sue and I set off along the seafront for a gentle Saturday afternoon stroll. It is some time since I last came to Budleigh but it is still the most peaceful and relaxing of seaside villages. It is remarkable that such an exquisite resort should have succeeded in remaining so unspoilt. There are a good number of retired residents (the average age of the local voters

must be nearer sixty than forty) and the only thing that breaks the silence is the tap tap tap of walking sticks and the rubberised shuffle of walking frames. There are no gaudy amusement arcades, and no noisy transistor radios. Budleigh (and indeed the same is true of the neighbouring town of Exmouth) has succeeded in remaining aloof from the commercial excesses of the 1980s. It stands like an elegant lady from the 1920s, untouched by progress; within sight of the future but firmly embedded in the past; surviving in. but not becoming part of, the final decades of the twentieth century. There are wooden beach huts, plenty of comfortable wooden benches and fishing boats galore pulled up on the shingle beach. their nets spread out to dry. There is no sign here of those two ubiquitous and destructive twentieth-century evils: plastic and electricity.

We were walking quietly along the sea front when suddenly the cliff on the landward side sloped down to ground level and there, some quarter of a mile out of the town, nestling on what looked like a reclaimed patch of estuary land, lay one of the most beautiful cricket grounds I have ever seen. The match, I found out, was a Devon League fixture between Budleigh Salterton 2nd XI and the Chudleigh 2nd XI, and although there were no spectators that I could see (there were, of course, a number of ladies busily occupied inside the pavilion doing things with plates and knives and, undoubtedly, mountains of Devon clotted cream, scones and strawberry jam) the teams were perfectly turned out. The batsmen had whiter shoes and pads than a good many professionals I have seen.

We walked slowly round the ground and watched a few overs. It was marvellous stuff the very meat of

English village cricket, enthusiastic and determined, but good tempered and companionable. The second eleven players were trying harder than many professionals but doing so without ever forgetting the nature of the game. The fielders chased each ball as though their lives depended on it, but found time to congratulate the batsmen who had inspired their breathlessness.

It was a true example of English village cricket at its very best: teenagers, one boy and one girl, were doing the scoring; the groundsman's tractor, mower, heavy motorised roller and two smaller rollers were parked neatly near a storage shed; the green and white painted pavilion (with green flag with golden otter proudly flying from the roof) still smelt of fresh paint; and the silence was broken only by the sound of birds singing, and the cries of cricketers at play (a splendid change from blaring car horns, banging tins, and mindless chants from senseless and prejudiced spectators). To the left, there lay a still river, its surface opaque with algae, and behind the ground a small, muddy brook. And a couple of hundred yards in front there lay the western edges of the English Channel.

Those of us who love cricket and watch it on the big city grounds sometimes forget that this is where it all started, that this is what cricket is all about, that whatever they may do at Lords or at Trent Bridge, at Melbourne or at Barbados, it will never ever be as important as what happens on elegant village greens in the Budleigh Saltertons of England.

Sunday 20th May

Three very good chums, Sir Bertie Wheezer, Dr Ambrose Crump and The Rev Horatio Smith all turned up in Budleigh Salterton to help celebrate my birthday.

All three are half-crazed cricket fanatics — Smith never travels anywhere without his bat, pads and a ball (he even took them to Italy earlier this year) — so an impromptu game was inevitable. After an excellent meal at the King William we made our way to the beach. Over lunch I had protested that the pebbly beach in this delightful part of South Devon is not well suited to the game of cricket, but no one seemed prepared to listen.

We played for ninety minutes before abandoning the match. It is difficult I to tell which was most difficult: trying to bowl on pebbles, trying to bat when the ball's course is entirely unpredictable, or trying to run when every step seems doomed to failure. Crump, who fielded up to his knees in the cold sea, was shivering and unable to talk coherently, so we went straight back to the flat. Hot tea and home-made ginger cake seemed to revive him quite quickly. Catering is so important in all classes of cricket.

Sunday 27th May
Despite my complaints about BBC 2's televised coverage of the John Player Special League matches, I settled down to watch the afternoon s. match with some enthusiasm. I had been planning to drive over to Edgbaston to watch the local derby match between Warwickshire and Worcestershire, but not even the Brumberella could have coped with the downpour at Birmingham. An afternoon in front of the television seemed an acceptable alternative.

My plans were foiled by the fact that the BBC had decided to fill their Sunday afternoon with women's athletics. I find it difficult to believe that anyone can possibly gain pleasure from watching flat-chested, overmuscled chromosomal freaks comparing abilities to hurl javelins and leap over hurdles.

I am convinced that the BBC has been infiltrated by dangerous dissidents.

Monday 28th May
In most parts of the, country the only cricket to be televised is that made available through the networks but up here in Yorkshire they love their cricket too much to allow their viewing habits to be dominated by national considerations. Today I found myself in a friend's house for just long enough to catch a few overs of the traditional Roses Match between Yorkshire and Lancashire.

I must have picked a good time to be passing for in the space of those few overs I saw the redoubtable Sidebottom take no less than three wickets. First he had Abrahams, the young and enthusiastic captain of Lancashire, magnificently caught by an agile fellow called Swallow. Abrahams is a fiercely determined captain who seems well equipped to take the pressures of captaincy. I remember watching a game just after he had taken over the captaincy; some young batsman whose name I now forget was within a whisker of reaching his maiden century when Abrahams decided to declare. It was a decision which must have taken courage as well as something of the essential ruthlessness that so many modern captains seem to lack. Anyway, Abrahams, this time the batsman rather than the captain, was the first to go. The next was David Hughes, the man who must by now be weary of being remembered outside his county only as the saviour of Lancashire in that legendary one-day final at Lords when they played until around nine o'clock in the evening. Hughes has always struck me as being an essentially careful batsman, but the game today had presumably reached a point where caution was no longer called for. He swished, swatted and swiped and was eventually caught by Kevin Sharp at extra cover.

The third of this august trio was the famous Jack Simmons. The man whose popularity among Lancastrians can easily be measured by the enormous sum they raised for his benefit. Again Sidebottom was the bowler, but this time it was Bairstow who took the catch. He seemed to make quite a meal of it, turning what looked like a fairly straightforward catch into a three act high drama.

And with the departure of the stout and doughty Simmons I took my leave of the television set and wandered out in search of the motorway. Why do not more local television companies fill some of their daytime schedules with cricket instead of low-quality imported soap operas?

Tuesday 29th May

At Old Trafford today Gordon Greenidge scored 186 not out, playing the West Indies against Lancashire in a one-day match, I wish I had seen that particular innings. I have tremendous respect for Gordon Greenidge who is, I feel, probably the most violently aggressive batsman playing in the world today. Admittedly past his best, he is still a man who can *punish* bowlers. He always, seems desperate to damage the ball as though it has offended him in some personal and unforgivable fashion. I remember once sitting high up in one of the stands at Edgbaston, in the rarefied area where they recently built their hideously named 'executive suite'. Greenidge, opening the batting for Hampshire with the great but sadly thwarted Barry Richards, sent one massive six high into the stand where it landed about a yard to my left on one of the concrete steps.

There was nothing particularly remarkable in that, but the ball landed with such force that it bounced straight back down onto the playing area, a distance of some fifty yards at the very least.

Wednesday 30th May

Before today I had never thought of umpires (apart from the odd one) as being driven by ambition. I had always thought of umpiring as something done by people too old or infirm to play the game (I excuse this attitude by admitting immediately that I consider myself not only too old and too infirm to play cricket but also too old and infirm to umpire).

My thinking about umpires (professional umpires at least) was changed by a play on BBC television this evening. Written by former Derbyshire player Peter Gibbs, and called *Benefit of the Doubt,* the play was centred around two main characters — both umpires. The older of the two was experienced, world weary, and apparently imbued with huge quantities of wisdom. Underneath, however, he was sadly cynical and essentially pragmatic in his approach to the game. His approach was perhaps best summed up when he admitted that although he would give a batsman out if he was boring to watch, he would always give the captain of any side the benefit of the doubt lest an uncomplimentary report about himself be sent to Lords.

The younger umpire, one of life's natural bank clerks, had been dragged out of his office and straight into the professional hurly-burly of a three-day county match. His attitude was summed up by a shot of him standing in front of the mirror practising holding up his index finger — and trying to look both convinced and convincing.

I found the younger umpire's attitude naive and rather pathetic. The older umpire's attitude I found depressing, and, in its way, equally pathetic. It is difficult to say how far these two rather exaggerated characters represent professional umpires in the modern game but one must assume that Peter Gibbs, as a former player, has some special knowledge. It does seem to me to be rather tragic that any umpire should put on his white coat expecting to go out into the middle to play an important part in the game. Good umpires, like good scorers and good groundsmen, should go unnoticed when they do their job properly. Indeed, I believe that the more an umpire attracts attention to himself then the worse he will probably prove to be. Good umpires need to be self effacing, and prepared to admit that their role, though essential, is supporting, not starring. The umpire who has failed to enjoy success at the highest level as a player and tries to make up for it by becoming some sort of celebrity as an umpire must end up taking himself and his role far too seriously.

I think W G Grace had it summed up perfectly. When an umpire overstretched himself enough to give the Great Man out, Grace pointed to the crowd, refused to move and explained: 'These people have paid to watch me play, not to watch you umpire'.

Thursday 31st May

I very nearly went to Manchester today to watch the first of the season's one-day internationals. But eventually I succumbed to sloth, abandoned the thought of driving north and settled in front of the television set to watch the match in peace and comfort.

Sitting at home one misses all the atmosphere but has the advantage of enjoying access to food prepared in style and avoiding those horrendous queues and parking problems that characterise watching high level cricket. These days it sometimes seems as though the police are determined to make things as difficult as possible for motorists anxious to find somewhere legal to abandon their motor cars. I would have thought that great sporting occasions, drawing exceptionally large crowds into areas ill-equipped to cope, would have represented suitable opportunities for authorities to organise Park and Drive services. Motorists could he directed to large public car parks, fields or whatever and then 'bussed' in the grounds.

With all the horrors of finding somewhere to park waiting for me in Manchester I decided, as I say, to stay at home and watch the match on television.

I wish I had gone to the ground.

Viv Richard's innings of 189 not out has been described as one of the best ever played in any class of cricket. It is, of course, impossible to compare innings. There are so many variables to be taken into consideration — the quality of the bowling, the nature of the pitch, the, state of the match and so on — that comparisons must be far too objective to be of any real value.

But I wish I had gone and seen it for myself. It was not just Richards who did the damage, of course. The last pair of batsmen put on a century between them and that is always discouraging for a team. Incidentally, I wonder why teams continue to play one-day cricket as though it were an entirely different game to first class cricket. I strongly suspect that if England had played this match aggressively, and had tried to dismiss the West Indians rather than merely contain them, they would have had a much better chance of avoiding that sort of last wicket partnership and of winning the match. The paradox is, of course, that when you try and stop a team scoring, rather than try and take wickets, then you put them under far less pressure and make it easier, rather than harder, for them to push the scoring rate along.

I say all this knowing very well that it is far easier to make positive, constructive suggestions from behind the safety of the boundary rope than it is to make similar types of suggestion when you are out there on the field of play and you have to translate ideas into action. There was a perfect example of this today provided by the television commentators.

During one fifteen-minute spell I am quite sure that I heard the same pair of commentators first of all suggest that Botham and Willis be brought on to bowl more or less immediately and then suggest that it would be better if they were kept until later. When Botham *was* brought on and he took a wicket the commentators praised themselves as though they had known exactly what was going to happen all along, and as though they were responsible for the success. If Botham had *not* taken a wicket they would, I suspect, have been quick to condemn the captain.

Friday 1st June
Minutes after I arrived in Nottingham this evening, ready for tomorrow's one-day international at Trent Bridge, a thunderstorm shattered the evening calm. It did not last long, however, and tomorrow's cricket should be quite safe. Not for the first time I felt a wave of sympathy for the groundsmen who have to look after wickets on major cricket grounds. I wonder if they stay up all night waiting to see if it rains and then checking

out the covers for leaks. Or do they go to bed, to be awakened only by the very loudest of storms?

I hope Dickie Bird is not umpiring tomorrow or else there will probably be a delay.

Saturday 2nd June

The start of today's one-day international was delayed for half-an-hour because of the thunderstorm the night before. I find it extremely difficult to understand just what difference thirty minutes is likely to make to a cricket ground. Dickie Bird is one of today's umpires and whenever a match I have looked forward to is delayed or abandoned, Dickie Bird always seems to be there. Mr Bird is, I am quite sure, a. conscientious and well-meaning umpire, (indeed I met him once at the Yorkshire TV studios in Leeds and found him to be a thoughtful and sensitive man), but not for the first time I wish I had some way of finding out in advance which umpires are due to officiate. I strongly suspect that if some sort of table were kept, Mr Bird would be found to be more sensitive to bad light and wet grass than many of his colleagues.

On the whole I think it is a pity that spectators are dealt with 'so shabbily by those whose living depends on the professional game. I know it is a little more dangerous than usual to play cricket in poor light or when the grass is wet but I do not see why cricketers need to be protected as though they were orchids in bloom.

Ironically, it seems to me that the more cricketers get paid, the more they complain about the risks of their sport. And yet if you look at other sports the risks in cricket are really very slight, and the dangers grossly over-emphasised. Sportsmen in other fields seem much more conscious of the needs of spectators.

You would not, for example, see skiers giving up just because the snow was a little icy or the mountain shrouded in some gentle mist. And yet their sport is infinitely more hazardous than cricket. To support my contention that cricket is not as dangerous as cricketers often claim I would point out that only relatively rarely do cricketers get badly injured. When was the last time you can remember a professional cricketer suffering anything more than a temporary knock or sprain? Modern cricketers are reasonably well paid for a relatively quiet and undemanding life. They really should be prepared to do a little more for their money.

Sunday 3rd June
Watched the Monaco Grand Prix on television this afternoon. Despite an astonishingly heavy thunderstorm the race went on as planned. The unfortunate drivers must have been driving blind for most of the race and judging by the number of accidents, they certainly had some terrible problems handling their cars on the watersoaked track. I could not help comparing the fact that whereas the Grand Prix went on as usual cricket matches these days seem to get cancelled for the slightest of reasons. If conditions are not absolutely perfect everyone stays in the dressing room rather than risk slipping and getting dirty flannels or a slight sprain.

Monday 4th June
The third and deciding match in the Texaco Trophy competition today. I know that cricket needs sponsorship money but I do wish that it would be just a little more discreet about it. I find it slightly offensive to hear international cricket fixtures, and even Test Matches, being talked about as though they were darts

tournaments or snooker competitions. Wimbledon still manages to distance itself from commercial sponsors and they have not yet started calling their Men's Singles the Texaco Men's singles or whatever.

At the rate we are going, Lords will be renamed Shellmex House by the end of the decade.

Thursday 7th June
According to today's newspapers, magistrates in Leicester have just turned down an application from the County Cricket Club there for all-day licences for the fifty-eight days of cricket due to be held at Grace Road this summer. The decision was clearly unexpected; Mike Turner, the club's secretary and manager; was reported to be 'almost speechless' — itself surely a comment on the controversial nature of the decision. There cannot be many things that could render the normally voluble Mike Turner 'almost speechless'.

I can quite see his point. Like it or not it is undoubtedly true that a good many people turn up at cricket matches because alcohol will be available all day long. Certainly, many of the companies which entertain their guests at cricket matches, hire boxes and marquees and, by their presence, ensure that there are catering facilities for vagabonds and wastrels like myself depend very heavily on the fact that they can allow their guests to marinate in beer and wine. A good many of the people watching first class cricket every summer do not know the difference between a googly and a gulley. But they enjoy the fact that beer flows from morning to evening.

Alcohol may produce much ill-mannered behaviour and may be partly responsible for the increasing rowdiness at cricket matches but, like it or not, it is the life blood of county cricket.

Saturday 9th June
Drove down to Worcester today to watch the game against Hampshire. Kapil Dev, the talented captain of India and all-rounder, made his debut for Worcester after long weeks of waiting. It must have been a difficult time for those who brought him to New Road and, indeed, for Kapil Dev himself undoubtedly anxious to prove his worth in county cricket after a fairly unhappy period at Northamptonshire. As it was, the debut was neither a disappointment nor a sensation. It will be interesting to see what sort of contribution Kapil Dev has made on the field by the time the season ends. From talking to players and officials, however, I rather suspect that even if he does not play in another match Kapil Dev will have made his mark on the Worcester players simply by being there. Introducing a world class player into a side has two useful side effects: it encourages all the other players to try a little harder, to prove that they are just as good and to make sure that *their* place is not at risk; second, it gives the team faith and confidence in its own ability to win competitions and trophies. So even if Kapil Dev himself fails to set New Road on fire, the enthusiasts who brought, him to the ground can count their patience and investment well worthwhile.

While at New Road I met John Inchmore who has now been told that he can, indeed, have a benefit next season. He was walking on air and already full of plans for raising money.

One of his first tasks is to form a committee to organise the benefit events and to delegate responsibilities to friends, relatives, club members and so on. One of the problems is that in order to minimise the risk of the Inland Revenue taking a close interest in the profits of the benefit fund it is important that the cricketer is not actually seen to organise anything. Can there be anything more absurd? The player must work in devious and roundabout ways: devising, suggesting and encouraging rather than overtly planning, arranging and collecting.

Inchmore is probably the archetypal county professional. He has served Worcestershire well over the last decade and has an excellent record with the club. He deserves a successful benefit.

Tuesday 12th June
When I was small, my father (who was not, I suspect, that fond of cricket) used to take me to Edgbaston to watch the Saturday's play in the Test. He used to write away for the tickets in January and between then and the allotted day I would think of little else. They were, as I remember, quite large, impressive looking, pinky-brown tickets and I used to check on their whereabouts quite regularly through the intervening months, concerned lest they be lost or stolen. I do not think I ever worried too much about it raining on the day; I would still have insisted on sitting there even if there had been twelve inches of snow on the ground.

It may be just the mystery and confusion caused by the passing of time but looking back it seems to me that going to Test Matches was infinitely more exciting then than it is today. Fences and railings along the roads and streets for miles around Edgbaston were covered with colourful hoardings and posters advertising competing national and local newspapers. We did not have a car park pass then and we used to arrive early so as to be sure to find a parking space. I remember that one year we parked in a private garden where an enterprising householder had let off his driveway and front lawn. Such commercial enterprise is probably frowned on; or may even be illegal, these days.

The hoardings may be gone. And I may have a car park pass already pasted onto my windscreen. But I am looking forward to seeing how England fare against this year's tourists.

Thursday 14th June
The other day I wrote complaining that Test Matches are not as exciting as they used to be. I was wrong. When I arrived at Edgbaston this morning, an hour early to ensure that I got into the car park, (where I intended to leave the car before going on to the Pebble Mill television studios for the first part of the morning), I found myself just as excited as I ever had been when I was small. The queues were already forming in the road outside the ground, and a small group of spectators were standing around the outdoor nets, waiting for a star or two to take a little pre-match practice.

The weather was hot and sticky, and the atmosphere felt oppressively heavy. The people I spoke to at the ground were convinced that the ball would move around but equally convinced that Gower, captaining England for the first time in a Test Match, would never dare emulate Denness and put the opposition in to bat. It seemed a toss to lose rather than win and the consensus of option among the people I spoke to was that England would probably find themselves batting whoever won the toss; the argument being that Lloyd, the more experienced and better established captain, being both further away from home and free of the spectre of Denness, *would* take a risk and invite England to bat.

In the end Gower won and, predictably and probably sensibly, decided to bat first.

As I had feared I finally spent the *whole* morning at the nearby television studios, recording the first of a series of programmes based on a recent book of mine, but the studio director kindly kept the monitor switched to the cricket as much as possible and I missed very little of the action.

People working in television and radio are invariably keen on cricket and whenever a match of any note is being played it is not difficult to persuade someone to switch on a radio or television set. I once did a one-hour live radio programme with an ear piece feeding me the Test Match Special commentary from BBC radio. By the time I arrived at the ground during the luncheon interval I was well aware that England had done relatively well to struggle to 73 runs for four wickets.

The main talking point on the ground, was of course, the fact that Andy Lloyd, a Warwickshire player appearing in his first Test Match for England, had been hit on the head and taken to hospital for tests and observation. It seems that the hapless batsman was just as much to blame for the accident as the bowler, since he had ducked into the ball rather than simply been hit on the head by a sharply rising bouncer. I do not know whether or not I missed any relevant announcement but as far as I am concerned it was not until the England innings closed later that afternoon, with just nine wickets down, that I finally realised that Lloyd was not coming back to bat. I thought it rather surprising that no public statement about his condition was made since a good many of the spectators, being Warwickshire supporters, were keen to know the extent of the injury and the condition of their young hero. The nature of the bowling can be judged, incidentally, by the fact that Botham, one of the most fearless and brave of batsmen, came out to the wicket wearing a white helmet. It is a long time since I saw Botham needing that sort of protection. Indeed it was not until late in the evening when Viv Richards and Larry Gomes were at the wicket that there were two batsmen in the middle *not* wearing helmets.

Apart from the cricket itself which was always fascinating if rather one-sided, two things about the day stuck in my mind as I drove homewards that evening.

First, there was the courageous and lively decision by the Edgbaston administrators to allow a West Indian steel band to play during the interval. I thought this was a tremendous idea for it gave the whole match a delightful carnival atmosphere. There was the added advantage that the band completely drowned the loudspeakers and so the dreary litany of instructions and exhortations which normally litter tea and luncheon intervals at Edgbaston was quite drowned out.

The second thing that stuck in my mind was the fact that someone had decided to increase the charge for scorecards from the usual fifteen pence to a staggering and quite outrageous twenty-five pence. How anyone can justify a charge of five shillings for a single sheet of rather cheap and badly-printed card I just cannot imagine. To add to this financial injury the scorecards these days are so heavily covered with advertising: material that there is hardly any space left on which to jot down the scores and bowling figures.

Saturday 16th June
Malcolm Mortimer telephoned from Nottingham today to tell me that he had managed to obtain tickets for the

Oval Test Match. Yesterday, apparently, he played on a pitch where there were large weeds growing on a good length. He tells me that a cricket ball pitched directly onto a dandelion can be expected to rise quite alarmingly. I tell him that England are in quite enough trouble already and to keep this information himself.

Sunday 17th June
The one memory that sticks in my mind about all the Tests I attended when I was a boy is of once sitting next to a man who had a scorecard which had been filled in entirely in pencil. My scorecard, which I had bought that day, had been partly filled in by the printers when I had bought it. My neighbour had clearly been at the match on the Thursday and the Friday too. I remember being terribly impressed by this, and wondering just what sort of man could take out three whole days to watch a Test Match, wanting to ask whether or not he was planning to attend on the Monday and the Tuesday too. And making a promise to myself that one day I too would attend all five days of a Test Match.

I was reminded of this when Gower decided to play safe and bat first in the Edgbaston Test. This in turn reminded me of the ill-fated match in which Mike Denness, who was captain, invited the Australians to bat. The Australians went on to amass a massive total and England lost the match. Denness was pilloried by the press for his audacity. It was that match that was the first I attended in its entirety. I remember that I sat through the whole of a wet and dreary Saturday and a gloomy Monday morning when the ground was emptier than it usually is for a three-day match, just so that I could satisfy that childhood ambition. We lost the match, of course, but it was a milestone in my cricket watching.

Since then I have watched several Tests and many county matches all the way through. Since I became a professional author I have done much of my thinking, planning and writing at cricket matches — and never failed to get pleasure from seeing every ball bowled, every run scored and every wicket that has fallen.

But this morning I decided not to go to Edgbaston on Monday. It is just too too sad to see a team being humiliated so I think I will stay at home and look forward to Lords.

Wednesday 20th June

The match between Yorkshire and Warwickshire that took place at Headingley today will surely count as one of the season's most exciting. Warwickshire, batting first, managed to amass a very reasonable total. The ageless Kallicharran (who is surely still a good enough batsman to be playing for the West Indies) helped create the basis of their score while wicket-keeper Humpage made the sort of contribution for which he is now quite rightly famous. The Yorkshire innings started with Chris Old managing to dismiss his former colleague, Geoffrey Boycott, and I doubt if anyone will take a wicket quite so sweet all season. I must confess that I was surprised that that was the only wicket Old took. All cricketers tend to try that little bit harder against their old counties and ex-Yorkshire cricketers usually have more incentive than most to do their very best. Still, perhaps the pleasure of dismissing Boycott was enough.

The finish, with Yorkshire needing just ten runs from the final over was nerve-racking. I very nearly missed it too. A middle-aged gentleman carrying rather too much weight and considerably too much beer collapsed a few yards away from me and I hurried across to see that all was well with him. As it was he had merely fainted in all the excitement and he came round in time for me to see Willis bowl an immaculate final over.

One of the perils of being a qualified doctor is that you are never really off duty. Even though I do not practise medicine any more I still feel obliged to respond when someone needs help. I really cannot begin to remember how many times I have knelt over prostrate spectators or soothed bruised and worried players.

Emergency calls to the pavilion are undoubtedly the most interesting of course. The problem with these is that if there are more than about a hundred spectators on the ground then you can pretty well guarantee that there will be at least half a dozen other doctors around. Turn up at the entrance to the dressing room and you find yourself queuing up alongside rows of general practitioners, orthopaedic surgeons, obstetricians, plastic surgeons, pathologists, psychiatrists and other assorted specialists. More surprising, perhaps, is the fact that the dressing room entrance will also be clogged up with bishops, philosophers, music doctorates and literary professors. I have never quite understood why they turn up but you can pretty well guarantee that when an appeal for a doctor goes out over the loudspeakers then anyone with any sort of doctorate will invariably turn up. Just what a doctor of divinity expects to be able to contribute is, I fear, a mystery to which I know no answer.

Over the years I have, I suppose, wandered into dressing rooms at most of the grounds in England. Apart from the very occasional battered batsman the problems are almost invariably at least fifty per cent psychological. Muscle strains, backaches, bruises and bouts of indigestion are the usual run-of-the-mill problem in the dressing room. Cricketers, like a good many professional sportsmen, whose ability to earn a good living depends very much on their ability to stay very fit, are fearful hypochondriacs, always dreading the worst, always convinced that they have just come off the field for the very last time.

Nor are team mates necessarily full of sympathy or understanding. I remember once struggling to examine a fast bowler suffering from what turned out to be gastritis. Throughout the examination, conducted on a wooden bench in the changing room, another bowler (later to win fame as an England player) insisted on using the wall just above my head as a target for throwing practice. They were not the easiest of circumstances. The bowler got some considerable relief from an antacid tablet I found lurking in a forgotten corner of my fishing bag. To treat the headache with which I left the dressing room I had to borrow a couple' of aspirin tablets from a kind lady in the sandwich bar.

Spectators, on the other hand, tend to be fairly seriously ill by the time they reach the point where they need medical help. Apart from the fact that you have to be a fairly hardened sort of character to spend cold summer days sitting on stark, uncomfortable wooden benches, spectators, who have paid to watch the game, tend to be reluctant to waste time being examined medically. When it is just hot or exciting, of course, there will usually be quite an epidemic of fainting. There may be an occasional heart attack or two as well. But when the cricket is fairly unexciting the problems vary enormously. Too much alcohol or too much food produce indigestion, headaches and vomiting. Bees, wasps and all sorts of other insects bite and sting. And during a particularly unexciting session I once found myself being consulted by a young couple who had asked the secretary to broadcast an appeal for a doctor because they wanted supplying with some form of contraception.

Oddly enough, however, the most frustrating experience I ever had as a cricket-loving doctor took place while I was listening to one of the Radio Three Test Match Special broadcasts. I was sitting comfortably in the garden, one delightfully warm Monday afternoon, listening to the closing stages of a very tedious match that had been heading for a draw since Friday lunchtime when suddenly, over the wireless, I heard the ground announcer's voice.

'If Dr J—— is on the ground would he please come to the rear of the pavilion.' went the announcement.

The second word of that announcement had set my heart beating a little faster. The third word of the sentence had calmed it down again. But a few moments later a second announcement was made.

'If there is a doctor on the ground would he please come to the rear of the pavilion.' Clearly Dr J had not responded.

After that announcement the time interval before the next was rather shorter. Whoever it was who had initiated the call was clearly beginning to panic a little.

'If there is a nurse on the ground would she please come to the rear of the pavilion,' said the announcer. (I apologise for the sexism in this comment but I am merely reporting what I heard.)

The final announcement, coming mere seconds after the third one was the most plaintive and desperate of all.

'If there is anyone on the ground with first aid experience would he or she please come to the rear of the pavilion as soon as possible?'

And after that there was silence. So either they found someone with first aid experience, or else the patient ceased to require the ministrations of a healer and became a problem requiring other hands.

Saturday 23rd June

I spent the afternoon today playing cricket down at Camberley. Surrey. Russell Smith, the friend I met at Lords earlier in the year, had invited a group down for afternoon tea and garden cricket. Although I suspect that the TCCB might have found the rules rather bewildering (a garden slide midway between the wicket keeper and the boundary and an immense oak tree at mid-on were just two of the more obvious variations on the traditional fielding theme) it was a delightful day.

Most people who have some love of cricket (players and spectators, professionals and amateurs) learn the rudiments of cricket while playing in a garden and it is easy, as one ages, to forget the simple but marvellous fun that can be had from a game under such restricted circumstances. There are local rules to be devised. If the ball bounces off the shed roof and is then caught, is the batsman out? If the ball is hit over the fence does that count as a four or six, and is the batsman out if the ball is lost? What are the rules if the dog picks up the ball and will not let go? How much energy is one allowed to expend while hunting for the ball among the dahlias? Are bouncers allowed? Is a soft ball or a hard ball to be used? Are there to be any special rules for female players? And, of course, there are all those unusual hazards to be faced: the bonfire, the compost heap, the greenhouse, the sundial, the overhanging apple tree branches, the bare patch where the fireworks have been let off or where the barbecue has scorched the grass and so on.

For most garden cricketers the biggest and most persistent problem is usually trying to ensure that the ball does not go into anyone else's garden. Down in Camberley the problem was exacerbated by the fact that anything hit a little uppish through the covers was almost certainly doomed to go straight over the fence. On the other side of the fence lay an immaculately manicured garden where there was absolutely no sign of human life but where a rather aggressive looking hound stood constant guard on the flower beds and lawns.

Inevitably, of course, just about every shot played went a little uppishly through the covers. Even when the bowlers sent each delivery down the leg side the batsmen still seemed unable to do anything other than send the ball flying between the fielders and over the fence.

Unable to take the time-honoured, respectable route towards retrieving the ball (a walk to the front door, a polite 'please may we have our ball back?' and a little furtive groping among the rhododendron bushes before an apologetic shuffle back past the kitchen window and out through the side gate) and unwilling to risk the less chivalrous route (sighting the ball, scrambling over the fence as furtively and quietly as possible, then scampering across the grass while keeping low and relatively invisible) we were left with only the third option: devising some form of contraption to retrieve the ball without setting foot in the garden.

In the end the combination which we found fairly successful consisted of a fairly soft rubber ball, four long bamboo canes, a bent safety pin and one and a half pairs of shoe laces.

And a large, succulent ham bone to keep the dog occupied.

Sunday 24th June
Over at Edgbaston today to watch a close John Player Special League match between Warwickshire and Somerset. I heard the news about the team selection for this Thursday's match at Lords.

Bravely, the selectors have put their trust in two newcomers, Martyn Moxon, the Yorkshire opener, and Chris Broad, another opening batsman but from Nottinghamshire. Neither are really 'young' in cricketing terms (Moxon is 24 and Broad is 26) but it does seem harsh to blood newcomers against the ferocious West Indian attack. I wonder if, before the series is over; the selectors will end up having to call on one or two of the older, forgotten men of English cricket? Surely there must be a Tom Graveney or a Cyril Washbrook to call upon for experience, style and courage? Quite a number of forty-year-olds have played Test cricket over the decades and looking around the English counties Dennis Amiss, Keith Fletcher, Alan Knott are all younger than Brian Close was when last he played for England. Unfortunately, none is currently fashionable enough to force their way back into the England side. There is, I suppose, always David Steele of Northamptonshire who had such a promising debut and such a short Test career. The unfortunate Steele only played in eight Tests and yet he averaged a very respectable 42.06. Both he and David Lloyd (the former Lancashire player who had a Test record very similar to Steele's) must wonder whether they would have had more Test chances if they had played for a more fashionable county. From the boundary's edge it is certainly difficult to understand why Mike Gatting, for example, has had so many more chances than these stalwarts.

The real irony about the new Test team is that the man who is probably the best English batsman in the game at the moment chose yesterday to remind the selectors, the team and spectators in general of his existence. When Graham Gooch scored a century against the West Indians not only was he the first player to do so but he was also the first English player to reach 1000 runs for the season. Gooch scored his century, by the way, off an attack which included Joel Gamer, whom the England side found virtually unplayable at Edgbaston.

Gooch was, of course, banned because of a trip he made to South Africa. I cannot help feeling that the truly outrageous nature of that ban has been highlighted this year by the fact that the Prime Minister of South Africa has been welcomed by our Mrs Thatcher, by the fact that a young South African girl has been given British citizenship so that she can run in the Olympics and by the fact that an English rugby team has visited South Africa. What really annoyed me. at the time was the realisation that Mrs Gandhi, who seems to have been partly responsible for Gooch and his team mates being banned, would never have dared to stop the Indian side playing against England. Indian cricket lovers tend to be rather volatile at the best of times. I honestly believe that if the Indian Prime Minister had tried to stop Test cricket between her national side and England (everyone's real cricketing enemy) then she would have been looking for some other form of employment.

The news about the team selection rather outshone the cricket at Edgbaston today. Look at the score-card and it will, I suppose, look as though it was a very close match. Indeed, it is true that right up until the last over Warwickshire *could* have won. But, somehow no one really thought that they *would* win. I really cannot explain this at all — perhaps it was a feeling that emanated from the players themselves, for somehow I suspect that the Warwickshire players did not really think that they could get the runs they needed.

The most interesting aspect of the cricket was, to be quite honest, the way that Ian Botham was received by the crowd. A year or two ago his appearance on the pavilion steps would have produced a huge roar of approval. Today when he came out to bat he was greeted by a remarkably restrained audience. It was even possible to detect a strange sort of communal embarrassment at his arrival. It was the sort of embarrassment one gets when a guest stays too long at a party. Or when an elderly but demented comedian or actor lives on for too long and makes a fool of himself on television in a desperate attempt to retain something of his former glory.

I think Botham's problem is that although he is still remarkably young (he is still two years short of his thirtieth birthday) he has achieved so much that he has become a real legend. Everyone knows that the man will rank among the game's all time greats, one of the most magnificent all-rounders the game of cricket has ever seen. That sort of status sometimes makes people feel slightly uncomfortable.

The other problem is, of course, that much publicised affair with the alleged but unproven use of drugs on last year's winter tour. A hundred runs and a few wickets in the next Test could easily banish all that from the public consciousness, of course.

Personally, my feelings about Ian Botham are very mixed. I admire his cricketing skills enormously. But I also feel tremendously sorry for him. How on earth he can possibly ever match those performances against the Australians I cannot possibly imagine. And it is, of course, those performances that people remember. I think he has done enough for England to be given a 'certain' place in the England side for just as long as he wants to play. But if success continues to elude him then I hope that he retires early. Botham has never been an ordinary cricketer and I would hate to see him become one.

Tuesday 26th June

When I told Sue that England were due to start another test match against the West Indies on Thursday she seemed rather puzzled.

'But I thought they'd played each other a couple of weeks ago,' she pointed out. 'and I thought the West Indies had won.'

She seemed surprised and rather confused when I explained that a Test Match was but one part of a series and that winning a single match was relatively unimportant, I have never really thought about this before but I *can* see that it must be difficult for people who do not understand cricket to accept that interest in a single contest can be spread over such a long period.

I refrained from pointing out to her that the contest with Australia has been continuing for over a century and that although *they* are currently winning, the match between us is likely to continue for another century at the very least.

Wednesday 27th June

Over the years I have heard a number of strange messages broadcast over the loudspeakers at cricket grounds. I have heard businessmen being summoned to their offices because of surprise visits by head office supremos. I have heard motorists being instructed to move their motor cars. I have heard small boys being instructed to meet fathers outside the bar. I have heard urgent messages from wives ordering their husbands home.

But all the messages I have ever heard have been for spectators. I have never before heard a message being broadcast for one of the players. Today, however, at Northampton, the announcer on the public address system told us that Mr George Sharp, the Northants wicket-keeper, had just become a father for the first time. Sadly, a few minutes later, Sharp was on his way to hospital himself Not to the maternity hospital I. hasten to add. He had been hit on the thumb by a ball from Wayne Larkins and needed X-rays.

Thursday 28th June

Fortune has dealt very different cards to the two young men who were picked to play for England today; Chris Broad has marked his debut with a magnificent 55 and seems to have secured one of England's opening batting spots for at least another couple of Test Matches. Poor Martyn Moxon, on the other hand, is currently nursing the ribs that were damaged just two days after his selection was announced. With Broad temporarily settled in the side it is now perfectly possible that Moxon will not have another chance to get into the team. He, like the unfortunate Andy Lloyd, could well end up having had fame and glory slip through his finger tips.

I had to spend the morning in television studios in Birmingham but the producer, Mike Dornan, kept the floor manager well supplied with scores and up-to-date details. I listened to the afternoon's cricket on the radio in my study. Brian Johnston was in excellent form. I wonder if any other broadcaster has ever managed to combine such a depth of knowledge with such an easy manner. Johnners carries his talent very lightly and makes an extraordinarily difficult job seem ridiculously easy. He epitomises everything that is truly English about cricket. There is noone broadcasting who comes close to him. Today I heard him tell how he had met the England newcomer Chris Broad and Broad had confessed that at the age of fifteen he had collected the broadcaster's autograph. (Johnston, inevitably, reported that he had now in turn asked Broad for *his* autographs) This slight but rather pleasant anecdote made me think about how difficult it must be for young cricketers moving into Test cricket for the first time. At fourteen, a young cricket fan will be at his most impressionable — a mere six years later he could be playing for his country and sharing a dressing room with the very men who were his heroes. It must be quite bizarre, for example, for a young fast bowler to suddenly find himself changing alongside Bob Willis, Dennis Lillee or Michael Holding, and, indeed, sharing the new ball with such heroes.

Incidentally, I saw from the scores in this morning's newspaper that one English batsman is continuing to have a good season. Graham Gooch smashed his way to 227 yesterday. According to the *Daily Telegraph*, when an ambulance went by the ground with its siren wailing one wag suggested that it was coming to collect the much punished and battered ball. I still cannot help wondering how different this Test series would have been if Gooch had been able to play.

Saturday 30th June
Botham has done it again. Just when *everyone* (myself included) had decided that he could not possibly dominate a Test Match in the way he had a couple of years ago Botham suddenly pulls out a genuinely world class performance. Only four bowlers have taken eight wickets for England at Lords. Botham is two of those cricketers. How long now before this young hero becomes Sir Ian Botham? It may seem unlikely but it is now surely quite inevitable.

Monday 2nd July
When the umpire offered Allan Lamb and Derek Pringle the chance to go off the field for bad light this evening I never imagined for a moment that they would accept the invitation. I thought the fact that the offer was accepted to be a considerable indictment of English cricket these days. I do not know whether the decision was made by Lamb and Pringle together or by just one of the players alone (if so then presumably Lamb, who had just scored his century). I gather from the news reports that Gower, the captain, had no influence on the decision.

It seemed to me to be a senseless and cynical decision for several reasons. First, it seemed to suggest to me as a mere spectator that the batsmen had decided that they had no hope of winning the match. At the moment when they chose to go off the field England were establishing themselves in a controlling position. If they had carried on batting (in the undoubtedly poor light) then they would have been able to accumulate more runs and give the West Indies a bigger target for the final day of play. For the first time for many months a team had managed to force its way into a controlling position against the West Indies. By leaving the pitch at that particular point not only did Lamb and Pringle take the pressure off the West Indians but they also allowed Clive Lloyd and his men to regain psychological control of the situation. The only possible reason for leaving the pitch was to avoid losing wickets — and that in turn meant that England were still worried about the possibility of losing the match. Psychologically that meant that all the initiative was back in Clive Lloyd's hands.

The batsmen's decision to leave the pitch disappointed me for another, very different reason. And that was that their decision to abandon the opportunity to pick up some additional runs also meant that the spectators were deprived of an entertaining session of play.

It is sometimes seems quite unfashionable among professional cricketers to regard spectators as being of any real significance at all. I cannot think of any other sport where the players seem to be openly contemptuous of the people who pay their wages. Golfers and tennis professionals rarely stop playing unless it's pouring down and even then they usually have to be dragged away from the course or court. Footballers play on in snow, hail, frost and rain — I have seen footballers playing in conditions so bad that it was impossible to see either goal mouth from the centre of the pitch.

But a high proportion of modern cricketers seem ready to walk off the playing arena at the drop of a hat. And this is desperately unfair on the paying spectators — the people who have paid the money that has made the game possible in the first place. Professional cricketers are, like all other professional sportsmen, entertainers. They get paid because people like to watch them perform. Watching as much cricket as I do, I sometimes get the uneasy feeling that there are cricketers around whose sole ambition is to be paid as much as possible for playing as little cricket as possible.

Whether this is true or not is to a certain extent irrelevant: what is relevant is that it is the way spectators sometimes see things. And without spectators prepared to pay money to watch cricket there will be no sponsors, no prize money, no benefits, no fat contracts and no professional cricket.

Allan Lamb and Derek Pringle might like to reflect on that the next time they are offered the chance to stop playing for bad light.

Tuesday 3rd July

As Gordon Greenidge powered his way to a magnificent 214 not out today I could not help thinking that the presence of the West Indian team here playing Test Matches does at least mean that a dozen or so English players will get the chance to play regular county cricket for a season. That in turn means that by the time the West Indians come here next we may be able to offer them a closer series.

I listened to today's play on the radio and it was amusing to hear all the experts changing their minds about the outcome of the day's cricket.

At 11 am all the commentators and experts were agreed that there were only two possible results: a win for England or a draw.

At lunch the commentators and experts were all agreed that the draw was the most likely outcome although one or two of the more optimistic former players argued that if the West Indies continued to go for a win it would increase England's chances of victory. (I think their argument was that while going for a win the West Indians would be more likely to lose wickets.)

By 3pm the commentators and experts were beginning to have doubts about England's chances of winning. The consensus of opinion was that the match would be a draw. Everyone was agreed that Greenidge had batted brilliantly and saved the day for his side.

By 4pm the commentators and experts were convinced that a victory for the West Indians was a foregone conclusion. A victory for England was clearly out of the question. A draw was considered equally unlikely.

I wish I had recorded the day's commentary. Recorded highlights and edited forecasts and predictions would have made an excellent short programme.

Friday 6th July

Most cricket captains, pundits, commentators and bar room experts will insist that if he wins the toss a captain should always choose to bat first. He might like to think about fielding and putting the opposition in to bat. He may even discuss the matter with the other players. But, in the end, he should always decide to bat first. However doubtful the pitch may be, however treacherous the local atmospheric conditions may be, batting first is, say the experts, the only sensible alternative. It is, they say, much safer to get your runs on the board than to end up having to bat last on a pitch that may be breaking up.

Today, talking to a friend of mine who plays all his cricket down in Somerset I heard of a captain who t always puts the visiting side in to bat. Never, in ten years of captaincy, has he chosen to bat first after winning the toss. And yet despite their captain's unusual approach to the game the team has won most of its matches.

The secret of the team's success is quite fascinating. It seems that the captain has some connection with a local cider company and before the match (as a welcoming gesture) he always puts a couple of barrels of his best 'scrumpy' in the visiting team's dressing room. His opening bowlers are then given fairly strict instructions to try to tie down the opening batsmen for a few overs but not to try too hard to take wickets.

The ploy apparently works like a charm. By the time the opening batsmen are back in the pavilion, numbers three and four on the opposition team are already beginning to feel the effects of the cider. While they stagger around in the middle for a few overs the opening batsmen can settle down to catch up on their team mates who have all been busy taking advantage of the local hospitality.

Whatever score the batsmen manage to put together, the home team, playing against bowlers and fielders who have little idea of just how to run let alone bowl, catch or throw, can usually better it in a relatively short space of time. Not that it is just the more obvious effects of the alcohol that cause the problems, my friend insists that he has seen five members of a visiting side queuing outside the clubs only earth closet. Crude country cider does have a rather spectacular effect on the human bowel.

This unsophisticated form of gamesmanship has proved remarkably effective. The only team to visit the village and not succumb consisted of eleven clergymen from a diocese in Bristol.

Perhaps Peter May and David Gower should try putting a cask of rum in the West Indians' dressing room.

Monday 9th July
For a long time now I have been desperately keen to get hold of an MCC blazer — one of those old fashioned ones in the traditional stripes of the club. I wrote off to the MCC shop at Lords and they have kindly put me in touch with an outfitters in London which will sell me one off the peg for about one hundred and forty pounds. I have started saving.

Wednesday 11th July
I spent the day watching Worcestershire play Warwickshire at New Road. To be perfectly honest I think it would have been more exciting if I had stayed at home and watched the grass grow and the garage doors warp. It was not an invigorating day's cricket. I did, however, have quite a fascinating time looking around at the various spectators. With nothing on the field of play worth watching I thought it might be entertaining to try to categorise cricket watchers. I came to the conclusion that a fairly limited number of basic categories can be defined. There are variations on these basic themes, of course. But most spectators can be slotted into one or other of these categories.

First, there are the spectators who are there for business. A growing number of firms seem to be discovering the business value of a day at a first class cricket match and these days the executive suites, directors' boxes and specially erected marquees are a regular sight on cricket grounds. The business spectators, or White Shirts, can be divided into two sub-groups. There are the hosts and the guests. The hosts always know a little about cricket and tend to have a ready fund of slightly threadbare cricketing anecdotes to tell. They can always boast a first name relationship with at least one player in the home side. The hosts are there to try and drum up business and so they always tend to be rather obsequious and to struggle hard to keep the conversation going throughout the day. The guests, on the other hand, rarely seem to know anything at all about cricket. They tend to ask questions like 'Are there eleven or thirteen in a cricket team?' and 'Do these fellows do this for a living or do they have jobs as well?'. Their questions are always treated seriously because the hosts hope to take some of their money off them before the day's play is concluded.

    Although the hosts and their guests are ostensibly on the ground to watch the cricket, the provision of plentiful supplies of food and drink is an important part of the day. The White Shirts tend to disappear into their marquee or special dining room at the very moment that the players troop off for lunch and they then tend to stay there until about twenty minutes before the tea interval. They make their absence noticeable by leaving behind a huge block of specially reserved seats upon which will be littered score cards, empty glasses, neatly furled copies of the Financial Times and expensively-printed cardboard folders containing literature about the host firm's favourite products. During the afternoon session the noise from the marquee or dining room tends to increase in volume as more and more alcohol is consumed. When business spectators wander back into their seats for the last couple of hours of play they will all be in shirt sleeves, although it will be rare for any of them to have removed their ties. Business spectators are never in evidence on Saturdays or Sundays, by the way.

(Just in case anyone is thinking of suing the for libel, may I point out that these observations are based not on one day's cricket at Worcester but on many years of cricket watching at dozens of different grounds,)

The White Shirts consume fairly large quantities of alcohol but the second group of spectators, the All-Day-Drinkers, make them look like temperance agents. The All-Day-Drinkers attend cricket matches because they know that the bars will be open from the bowling of the first ball to the close of play. And they take full advantage of this loophole in our otherwise stringent licensing laws. Usually favouring beer they try to sit as near as possible to the bar and they generally form some sort of rota system to bring supplies out to their seats.

This means that one spectator can often be seen unsteadily making his way from the bar carrying two trays and perhaps a dozen pint mugs filled with beer. His colleagues will invariably cheer his progress and moan lightheartedly as he spills their drinks. This ritual, carried out by a different member of the rota each time, continues at roughly half-hourly intervals throughout the day.

The All-Day-Drinkers tend to get very boisterous by early evening. They usually know a good deal about cricket but the value of what they say tends to vary in inverse relationship with the loudness in which those comments are made. During the morning sessions, when their blood alcohol levels are relatively light, the All-Day-Drinkers tend to be fairly witty and able to discuss the cricket with knowledge and understanding. They tend to converse fairly quietly, with only an occasional guffaw to hint at what is to come. By mid afternoon the All-Day-Drinkers have lost their reticence and are prepared to share their comments with anyone on the ground who is not actually stone deaf. Unfortunately, by this time the beer, which has given them the confidence to shout, will have taken away their ability to think coherently. They will invariably offer a good deal of senseless advice to batsmen, fielders and umpires. It is the All-Day-Drinkers who sit at square leg and comment loudly on LBW decisions and who start slow handclaps if an over goes by without a six being hit.

The All-Day-Drinkers are fairly faithful cricket watchers but they do not usually turn up when the weather is foul or looks unpredictable. That cannot be said of the third group of cricket watchers — the retired spectators. These are recognisable not only by their age but also by the fact that they always wear woolly waistcoats underneath their suit jackets (even when the weather is boiling hot), and carry thick old-fashioned gaberdine raincoats with them at all times. They have old shopping bags by their sides which contain vacuum flasks full of tea and plastic boxes packed with cheese-and-tomato sandwiches wrapped in elderly, much creased greaseproof paper. Always sitting in the same seats the retired spectators or Woolly Jumpers will usually sit alone, although occasionally they sit in twos and share one another's sandwiches.

At the other end of the age spectrum there are the schoolboy spectators. These fall into two very distinct categories. First, and rarest, are the groups of boys in smart blazers and expensive school ties. Usually accompanied by a school teacher, these young Blazer Boys always troop into the ground in a neat crocodile and they always sit and chatter among themselves.

They will very often go home at four o'clock when the school day is officially over.

The second type of schoolboy spectators (Tennis Ball Boys) are the ones who come to the ground equipped with autograph books, scorecards and cricket bats. These are the true enthusiasts. One or two of them will eventually earn some sort of living out of cricket: many of them will continue to play with cricket clubs when they leave school, most will retain an affection for the game and will end up joining the club as members when they grow up. These youngsters, usually wearing jeans and anoraks, invariably carry large sports bags and huge plastic bottles full of orange juice or some other similar cordial. Throughout the match they pay careful attention to the play and comment knowledgeably on the skills exhibited and on the wisdom of the captains as they switch their bowlers around. During the luncheon and tea intervals they rush out onto the pitch, carrying their bats and an old tennis ball. There they exhibit skills of varying worth but an undimmed level of enthusiasm. At the close of play they all rush onto the pitch and surround the players, asking for autographs. Most will hang on for some time after the close of play, waiting for players to leave the dressing room. The undiscriminating will collect autographs from anyone carrying a cricket bag or looking bronzed and fairly fit. The discriminating know just which autographs they need to complete a set and which are worth collecting as 'swaps'.

I always feel very strongly that these young spectators are the lifeblood of English professional cricket. It annoys me to hear them being bullied by gatemen, harassed by petty administrators and snapped at by other spectators. When there are no longer any young boys with tennis balls making a nuisance of themselves on the outfield, we can all start to worry about the future of cricket in England. Until then the future is in safe hands.

The next group of cricket spectators are the Statisticians. These are usually (but not always) male. They always have large score books on their knees and current copies of *Wisden* on the bench beside them. They keep a careful record of every ball bowled, every run scored and every wicket taken. They can provide a fairly useful service to other spectators but they can, occasionally, be a little tedious when they insist on sharing information. I am not too keen to know that I have just seen the fastest fifty ever scored by a forty-year-old left-handed bald batsman on the second afternoon of a three-day match in late June.

Similar in number to the Statisticians but very different in every other way are the Cricket Groupies. These are a relatively new addition to cricket watching and they are by far the prettiest of all (except perhaps for the secretaries and publicity assistants who invariably accompany the host business spectators and whose job it is to entertain and distract those guests who find leg slips and maiden overs too uninviting a distraction).

Cricket Groupies are always female (as far as I have been able to ascertain), usually between the ages of fourteen and twenty-four and sometimes quite staggeringly beautiful. They tend to sit near the boundary and usually favour those spots where their heroes can be found fielding. Invariably bra-less, they flaunt their best points unashamedly. To attract Cricket Groupies you have to be young, internationally renowned and fairly flamboyant. Fast bowlers seem to be most likely to find themselves surrounded by Groupies although all-rounders and hard hitting batsmen do quite well too. I do not know whether it is the television exposure or the high salaries paid to some cricketers that attract Cricket Groupies. I suspect that it is probably a combination of both. Whatever the reason for their presence, I would certainly like to know what some of the cricket Greats would have to say to the idea of being surrounded by Groupies at the end of a match.

Can you imagine W G Grace coming off the field to find a bra-less, busty, raven-haired beauty in a mini skirt throwing herself at him? The Grand Old Man would have had a fit.

I have left the biggest group of spectators until last. These are the spectators who really keep professional cricket alive. They are the individuals who turn up to watch county cricket when Northamptonshire are playing Lancashire to decide who is fourteenth and who is fifteenth in the County Championship Table; the people who turn up whether it's sunny or raining, and who sit there patiently while the umpires look at the pitch, stare at the sky and exchange confidences for the third time with the assistant groundsman.

The one thing that these spectators have in common is that they go to cricket matches for a little peace and quiet. They go there to get away from the hurly burly of modern life, to find time to think, to rest and to relax, to escape from telephones, traffic and nagging wives, and to soothe themselves with a day's pleasure at a cricket match. These spectators, (Escaped Prisoners) enjoy their cricket, of course. They get a good deal of pleasure from watching a good, tight game or seeing a batsman or bowler excel. But they get something much, much more from their cricket watching. They unwind as the day goes by and you can almost see the tension draining from them. They read the paper a little, do a crossword at lunchtime, read a few pages from a book they have brought with them, chatter occasionally to a few friends, smoke an occasional pipe and enjoy a couple of pints of beer. They eat a pie, a scotch egg and a beef sandwich at lunchtime and have an apple, a piece of fruit cake and a cup of tea in the middle of the afternoon. They get there early in the morning and they stay there until the close of play. They usually turn up alone or with a couple of chums (their wives invariably find the game boring and stay at home; which is just as well because if their wives did not find the game boring then they would probably have to switch to fishing for a hobby). They take a few days holiday for a Test Match and one or two county matches and occasionally sneak away to a day's cricket on the pretext of having a bad back or a mild touch of flu.

There are, of course, some cricket spectators who turn up just when there are big matches planned or simply for the excitement of a one-day close encounter. These cricket spectators (Casuals) undoubtedly bring money into the game and get great pleasure from their cricket watching. But they are not *real* cricket spectators.

They would not turn up at New Road to watch Worcestershire and Warwickshire on a humid Wednesday afternoon in July.

Thursday 12th July
I always enjoy going to Worcester. It is such an extraordinarily friendly ground. At lunchtime and teatime and after the end of play young spectators crowd onto the pitch to play their own private games of cricket. Older spectators clamber over the fence to have a lie down on the outfield. And however many people

there are on the grass, I do not think I have ever heard a single word of admonishment or warning over the loudspeaker system. I honestly think that is one of the reasons why the ground feels so welcoming and friendly.

At some grounds (and Edgbaston is, I am afraid, one of the worst offenders in this respect), I have sometimes listened to the instructions coming over the loudspeakers with a mixture of embarrassment and rage. Some of the men hired to use the loudspeaker seem to me to be insufferably officious; rather like ageing schoolmasters who have long since run out of patience. Their patronising, arrogant, conceited bleatings make visitors and members alike feel like unwelcome intruders. I have heard small boys told off for hanging their coats over the advertising hoardings, and young cricketers praised for leaving the pitch neatly, orderly and quickly. It is hardly surprising that most cricket matches are played on almost empty grounds.

At Worcester I have never heard a cross or impatient word over the loudspeakers. I have seen the players coming back onto the pitch and playing a quick game of catch with youngsters finishing off their own impromptu games, and I have seen play commence with a dozy spectator still stretched out at third man, quite unaware of the fact that play had started.

And yet none of this friendliness has ever adversely affected the cricket. Players do not suddenly find themselves struggling to fight a way through hordes of ill-mannered spectators; the groundsman does not have to contend with hundreds of feet stamping all over his wickets; the umpires do not get molested or even catcalled; and the turf does not get badly damaged. The crowds at Worcester are invariably contented, happy and well-behaved.

I wish the same could be said of all those grounds where the loudspeaker announcements are occasionally tinged with acid, and where the spectators are kept off the pitch and well away from the wicket.

I do not care what the match is, I believe that spectators always have a right to wander onto the grass, to play their own small games of cricket (with a soft ball, of course, since with a few dozen minor matches in progress it is not always possible to see which balls are going where) and to hang their coats over the railings. I for one shall continue to spend most of my cricket watching days at grounds where these simple rights are respected.

I go to cricket matches to rest and relax.

I always feel good at Worcester and I drove home from the ground this evening feeling full of love and affection for what must surely be one of the most attractive cricket grounds in the world.

Friday 13th July

This is the third time this year that Friday has landed on the 13th of the month. And, as ever, I stayed in for the day. I am incurably superstitious. I spent some of the day sitting in the garden listening to the Test Match commentary on the radio and part of the day watching the television transmission.

As I think I have already argued this year, I do think, that the quality of cricket commentating is deteriorating. It is difficult to say exactly why this is, but I suspect that one of the problems is that producers seem intent on hiring just about every ex-cricketer who is available. I cannot think of any other sport where professional players are so well represented among commentary teams. The theory seems to be that if one is going to have useful and acceptable commentary then one must have former Test players in front of the microphone. This really is extraordinary nonsense. In other sports professional commentators and correspondents predominate: in cricket the former players fill up an ever increasing percentage of the air time. It is easier to make a list of the Test players who have not commentated than to make a list of those who have. There are three main problems with this.

First, good as they may have been as players, many of these current commentators are barely articulate when talking about the game. They constantly litter the commentary boxes with clichés, ugly, grammatical errors, malapropisms and silly little pet sayings that add nothing at all to the listener's understanding or enjoyment of the game. My own former hero Trevor Bailey is as guilty as anyone of these sins.

The second problem with players masquerading as commentators is that they are often more interested in their own past than in the game they are supposed to be watching. One player who falls into this category is dear old Fred Trueman. Now Fred was a magnificent bowler and he is a great raconteur, but he does tend to get carried away a little when he is commentating. He seems to complain and moan far too much and not enjoy modern cricket at all. I cannot imagine why he allows himself to be paid for watching it. Actually, Fred Trueman is a rather interesting character. I spent a few fascinating hours talking to him up in Glasgow earlier this year when he visited the television studios there to take part in a programme on which I had a small regular spot. When he was a player the younger Fred was something of a fiery character quite often getting into trouble with the cricket authorities and not particularly well known for his love of committees. The older Fred is a rather different character, constantly complaining that today's cricketers have too little respect for their elders and betters and quick to criticise the modern professional, both at county and international level.

The third problem with allowing cricketers to commentate is that not all have good voices for radio or television. Take Mike Denness, for example. If you have heard him commentating you will know exactly what I mean. Would Mr Denness have ever been considered for a job on the radio if he had not played for England? I very much doubt it, I just cannot bear to listen to him.

All this is made more inexplicable and unforgivable by the fact that ex-professional cricketers also tend to watch cricket with different objectives to the ordinary listener.

You do not have to have played cricket to enjoy it, and the art of cricket spectating is something quite different to the art of playing the game. It is not necessarily an inferior art. The interest, demands and expectations of the former player tend to differ considerably from those of the professional commentator or spectator: the man whose only qualifications are a love of the game and a gift with words. You do not need to have played cricket to enjoy it or to describe what is happening.

Former players should continue to sit in the commentary boxes for both television and radio broadcasts. Their expert observations are fascinating and enlightening; simply because they are noted from a different, more perspicacious angle. But producers need to maintain the traditional balance by ensuring that there are always a good number of non-players on the commentating staff: men who are hired because they do something well, and not because they used to do something else well.

Saturday 14th July

It was good to see Malcolm Marshall come out to bat with his left hand in plaster. I know it's crazy, but somehow one expects one's cricketing heroes to be superhuman and to bat and bowl however badly they may be incapacitated. Colin Cowdrey became an English folk hero when he went out to bat at Lords with his arm in plaster. The fact that he did not have to face a ball is quite irrelevant: it was his presence at the crease that was all important. I suspect that in years to come Marshall's heroics here at Headingley will earn him similar immortality. I gathered afterwards that Marshall decided to go out to bat so that Larry Gomes, who was running out of batting partners, could get a much deserved century. If that is true it makes his gesture even more gallant.

Being at Headingley again reminded me of the day last summer when I came to the ground with a photographer from the *Yorkshire Evening Post.* There was no cricket being played but I spent a silly half hour posing in front of the scoreboard and grinning inanely at the camera. All this was to help promote a book of mine called *Thomas Winsden's 136th Cricketing Almanack* — an out-and-out spoof of Wisden itself

The cover of the spoof looked very similar to Wisden, but the contents were rather less earnest. I included details of the Australian Beach Cricket Championships, the new French Cricket rules and the scores from the amazing Curry Cup held in India last winter.

I put in details of the world's very first, genuine single wicket competition (it really was a single wicket competition and the bowlers had a simply terrible time), a technology section explaining how the Ball Speed Assessor works, and a remarkable story about cricketers swapping shirts at the end of the match in the same way that footballers do.

Since the original *Wisden* always gives a good deal of space to statistics, I naturally included a large statistics section. I put in details of the first Umpires' Averages Table and a unique Sandwich Making Averages Table. This showed that although cheese-and-tomato sandwich makers dominated club cricket, Mrs Pettifer, the winner, was a specialist in egg and cress. (She was present at 36 matches, made 1482 sandwiches, had the highest match score of 112 and ended with a magnificent average of 42 sandwiches eaten per match.)

I included details of the German tour to France in 1916, hints on clapping for the elderly and the inebriated and, for women cricketers, instructions on how to run without waving your arms about and how to knit a ball and stump cover. There were instructions on how to make a cheese sandwich, tips for the twelfth man (always hold the tray with your thumbs pointing towards the pavilion) and a whole chapter on chewing gum relics. There was even a section on illnesses affecting cricketers (pushed hamstrings, testimonialitis and soggy white skin from staying in the bath too long), and there were notes on what umpires carry in their pockets.

Writing all this nonsense was tremendous fun but promoting the book was even more fun. Apart from sitting sunning myself underneath the Headingley scoreboard, I spent much of the summer wandering around the country talking about *Winsden* and trying to explain why the other one hundred and thirty-five editions of his Cricketing Almanack had never appeared.

I cannot remember now all the interviews I did but I do remember being at Yorkshire TV studios one evening, sitting showing Richard Whitely some of my chewing-gum relics and showing him how my Bowling Machine worked, then racing down to London to spend the early morning sitting on the TVam sofa in cricket whites, showing Nick Owen my prototype Toxteth's Little Nipple Guards and trying hard to keep a straight face as I talked about the sandwich-makers averages with an increasingly incredulous floor manager standing nearby.

All in all *Winsden's Cricketing Almanack* was very well-received everywhere except at Radio London where a chubby little fellow, whose name I now forget, refused to interview me and made it very clear that he thought the whole thing to be in the worst possible taste. I do not suppose he will like this book much either.

Sunday 15th July
A fellow sitting near to me at Edgbaston today became very argumentative and started offering odds against Warwickshire managing to score 200 runs before being dismissed or before running out of overs. When I declined his offer of a bet he suggested that I might like to take two-to-one odds against any single Warwickshire player scoring 100 or more.

His third suggestion involved the total number of no balls he thought the Warwickshire bowlers would contribute to the total.

I refused all these offers but, inspired by that fatal combination of boredom and alcohol, the betting enthusiast seemed unwilling to give up so easily. He seemed quite desperate to arrange some sort of financial confrontation. So, for odds of twenty-to-one in pennies, I offered to forecast the score of every player in the two teams who had a chance to get to the wicket.

The betting enthusiast seemed scornful of my offer, making it pretty clear that he thought he would be taking money from me quite unfairly. He pointed out that batsmen can score anything between nought and 200 or even more and said that if I insisted on making such a reckless offer then he would at least want me to accept odds of thirty-to-one.

I accepted. And at the end of the day I had made a profit of seventy-six pence.

I must try this simple trick more often. The first person who tried it was, I think, an England player on a tour to New Zealand way back before the turn of the century. He won a fair amount of money from the local enthusiasts but ended up in prison when the losers complained (quite unreasonably I think) that they had been duped. If memory serves me right he was a wicket keeper and England spent some time on their tour without a specialist behind the stumps.

All I did, by the way, was predict a score of 'nought' for each player.

Monday 16th July

I thought that today's England batting collapse (the Fleet Street newspapers must have those three words permanently in type) was particularly pathetic. Anyone who worked in a factory, a shop or a bank and who worked with the sort of dedication and determination displayed by most of the England team this summer would be joining the dole queue by now.

The most extraordinary feature of an otherwise eminently forgettable match was the bowling of Malcolm Marshall, the new one-armed bandit of West Indian cricket, who somehow managed to take a career-best seven Test wickets despite having a fractured thumb encased in plaster of paris. You might have imagined that having a huge chunk of heavy plaster on his left hand would have disturbed Marshall a little unbalanced him perhaps. But it did not seem to have any bad effect at all. Indeed, since Marshall achieved career-best figures in this innings it is difficult to escape the conclusion that the heavy plaster may in some way have helped. Perhaps Marshall should have a similar plaster fitted onto his left arm for every Test Match. And maybe all England's bowlers should consider having their non-bowling hands encased in plaster of Paris.

Marshall, by the way, is taking part in the single wicket circus event due to take place in Somerset in mid-September. Malcolm Marshall, together with Ian Botham, Kapil Dev, Clive Rice and Richard Hadlee will be bowling at one another in an attempt to find the world's premier all-rounder (they will not all be bowling at once, of course, although it might be rather fun if they were).

Incidentally, a good friend of mine who is a keen Lancashire League cricketer suggested to me the other day that the single wicket rule might be introduced into club cricket in an attempt to ensure that all players in a team get a better chance to take a real part in the game. Too often keen but unexceptional club cricketers look forward to their Saturday match only to have a couple of overs bowling at most and never get a chance to bat at all. My friend's suggestion was that each player in a club side should be expected to bowl a minimum number of overs and also be allowed to bat for a fixed number of overs. The team's success would then be measured by dividing the total number of runs scored by the complete side by the total number of times that the side had been dismissed.

This may be a suggestion designed to offend the purists but it would give an awful lot of club cricketers a good deal more pleasure in their everyday games.

Tuesday 17th July

I wandered down to Fleet Street today to discuss a book serialisation with Robert Wilson, a friend of mine and editor on one of Britain's leading newspapers. When I arrived I was surprised to see that he had his right arm in plaster. Since it meant that he could neither hold a glass nor sign his expense chits this was obviously a tragedy of some importance. I asked him how it had happened.

With some bitterness he told me that a cricket club in Kent, of which he is an enthusiastic amateur member, had recently decided to encourage its playing members to take up a regular exercise programme. Wilson insisted that up until six months ago the only exercise he ever took was either in the pub or on the cricket field. This, however, was all changed by the Club President who, having watched the England cricket team going through their paces some months previously, had decided that a full programme of physical exercise would improve the overall fitness and performance of the players. To ensure that the exercise programme was well organised and adhered to rigidly the President managed to persuade a local aerobics teacher to turn up in the nets twice a week and pass on some useful hints.

According to Wilson, this well-meant attempt to turn the team into active, agile athletes proved to be the club's undoing. Unused to cavorting around in track suits, touching their toes or waving their arms about, the team suffered an astonishing series of medical mishaps.

The wicker-keeper and one of the opening bowlers strained thigh muscles in March and missed the first two months of the season. The club's most consistent player, a much experienced Lancashire League batsman accustomed to opening the batting and averaging over fifty, walked out in a huff after rupturing himself while trying to throw a medicine ball to the club's only spinner. The spinner acquired a broken toe when he tripped over a paving slab while out jogging and the only reserve wicket keeper had a heart attack trying to do too many press ups. The President was one of three players who developed forms of tennis elbow.

Of all the injuries, however, my friend's was undoubtedly the strangest. He was mugged while jogging near home and while trying to protect his face was hit fiercely by a very hard wooden truncheon.

'Last year,' said Wilson dolefully, 'I don't think any member of the team missed a match through illness. This year we've had to borrow players from visiting sides for most of our matches.'

He added that in his view tracksuits should all be marked with a Government health wanting.

Wednesday 18th July

Today I watched Warwickshire defeat Shropshire in the Nat West Trophy with mixed feelings. As a

Warwickshire supporter for thirty-odd years my primary loyalties were, of course, with the home team. But I have to admit that I felt a sneaking admiration for the minor county side. It is always strangely invigorating to see a giant killer doing well and the way that Shropshire trounced Yorkshire in the previous round of the competition must have delighted and entertained cricket lovers all over the country.

I cannot help feeling that the pundits who argue that there ought to be more cricket played between the first class counties and the lesser teams must have a valid point. I think this sort of mixed cricket helps everyone. It gives the amateurs and semi-professionals who make up minor county and league teams a chance to try out their skills against the household names. That cannot be a bad thing at all. The fact that the first class counties usually win proves that there is a difference between the top professionals and the very best amateurs. The fact that occasionally a minor county can win proves that the difference is not all that great.

Just how much more of a link there ought to be between the first class counties and the leading minor county sides is something that is much more difficult to decide.

The success of the minor counties in the Nat West Trophy and the Benson and Hedges competition does suggest that there might be some sense in allowing the leading minor county sides (1 am thinking of teams such as Durham, Hertfordshire and Oxfordshire) a chance to compete in the John Player League on a regular basis., Perhaps, for example, the winners of the Minor County Championship could be entitled to join the first class counties in the Sunday League for the following season.

This would obviously be far more sensible and practical than allowing part-time players to take part in the three day County Championship games. Not only is the divide between minor counties and first class counties more noticeable in this type of cricket, but the simple fact is, of course, that many minor county players would be unable to get time off work to play in such a competition. The only way to introduce this type of new blood into first class cricket would be to convert one of the minor counties into a full-time first class county, either increasing the number of counties to eighteen or downgrading one of the existing first class counties. I do not think that is a likely prospect.

I read in today's *Daily Mirror* that, according to Malcolm Marshall, the one English batsman they fear is Graham Gooch. I suspect that the West Indians are wise to be worried about Gooch for I think he could make a huge difference to the strength of the England side when the ban is lifted. England without Gooch is a bit like the West Indies without Viv Richards or the Indians with Sunil Gavaskar.

The other interesting thing that Marshall had to say concerned all-rounders. He argued that the English selectors are far too keen to fill their side with all-rounders, forgetting that to be a Test class all-rounder a player should be able to hold his place both as a batsman and a bowler. Some of the all-rounders England has tried in recent matches have been only moderately competent batsmen and only moderately competent bowlers.

Incidentally, looking through the averages which have been published today I see: that the country's leading all-rounder is one Graham Gooch. He is not only near the top of the batting averages but is also quite well placed in the bowling averages.

Thursday 19th July
I believe they organise cricket fixture lists with the aid of a computer these days and I suspect that it may be the same computer that keeps sending me the wrong gas bill, and keeps trying to persuade me to pay my TV rental company money I paid them a year or more ago. I looked in my diary today to see when I could slip over to Worcester again and I see that there is not a match at New Road until the 4th of August. The last first class match they played there was the fixture between Warwickshire and Worcestershire last week. A three week period in the middle of the summer with no first class cricket just is not good enough.

Friday 20th July
We used to call them 'donkey drops' at school but I do not know whether or not this was just a regional name. The more formal term is 'lob' bowling, of course, and there was a time when it was a fashionable and successful bowling technique. Having watched several thousand overs of routine medium pace this season it suddenly occurred to me today that it would be pleasant to see someone bowling 'lobs' or 'donkey drops' again.

The only underarm bowling that has been seen in top class cricket recently was, of course, that now disreputable Test Match incident when Trevor Chappell bowled underarm to stop a New Zealand batsman scoring a six and winning the match off the last ball of a match.

He bowled what we used to call a 'grub hunter' or 'daisy cutter' but I cannot help feeling that a proper lob bowler specialising in skilfully-flighted 'donkey drops' could tear through most first class cricket sides.

Just how would a professional batsman cope with a ball coming straight out of the air? The typical modern batsman has a very high backlift that would mean he would be more likely to hit the ball with the back of his bat than with the blade. You can't cut, sweep or drive a ball coming down over your head and straight at your stumps. You could, I suppose, hook a donkey drop if your timing was immaculate but a little change of pace would make that a very risky business indeed.

If you have ever watched a skilled boule player in France you will know that it is perfectly possible to send a ball up very high and get it to land on a fairly small target. So, a skilled lob bowler would be able to ensure that a batsman had to play at his deliveries. But once he had played at the delivery the batsman would be at considerable risk of getting a top edge or simply skying the ball to one of the close fielders. There would also be a very good chance of persuading the batsman to step back onto his wicket.

One other advantage of lob bowling occurs to me: there would be hardly any LBW decisions. Umpires would surely welcome that!

Saturday 21st July

Down at Lords to watch Warwickshire play Lancashire in the Benson and Hedges final I cannot help thinking of the NatWest final two years ago when Warwickshire lost in such a humiliating way to Surrey.

I spent a day watching that match from the top balcony of the pavilion — surely one of the best places in the world from which to watch cricket — and can remember vividly one particular encounter that took place before the cricket even started.

I had established myself in a comfortable spot, right above and behind the bowler's arm, a little before ten.

Even then, however, there were quite a number of spectators gathered along the white-painted benches there. Three of them in particular caught my eye. Indeed it would have been difficult to ignore them. They were all enormous— over six feet in and weighing an average of fourteen or fifteen stones I should think. They had brought with them two huge cool boxes filled with bottles of champagne, expensive-looking cheeses and fine pâtés. They were immaculately dressed, hugely muscled and looked as if they probably did something marginally illegal for a living.'

Suddenly, as if from nowhere, a tiny little man in a long grey raincoat appeared directly in front of them. He had neatly slicked back thinning hair, a thin toothbrush moustache and a tiny, weasel-like face.

'You can't sit there,' he squeaked. 'That's where I sit. I always sit there.' He was pointing at all three as he spoke.

'Sorry mate,' said the biggest of the three men, putting down the glass of champagne that he had just poured himself and leaning forwards slightly. He spoke in a broad cockney accent. 'Sorry mate, but we've bin ere since arf parst noine. '

'But that's my seat' protested the weasel. He looked and sounded like the archetypal petty administrator.

'Sorry mate' said the champagne drinker, with a sniff.

'I'm on the committee here,' protested the weasel. 'I'm going to complain about you. You'll get into trouble. That's my seat.'

I looked across to the three men with the champagne bottles the cheese and the pâté. They looked very well settled and I really couldn't see them being unnerved by this threat.

'Look 'ere mate,' said the spokesman, slowly unwinding and standing up. Because he was on a higher tier than the weasel he had to bend almost double to get face to face. 'If you don't go away and leave us alone I'll frow you over the balcony.' And with that he sat down.

The weasel-faced administrator opened and shut his mouth a couple of times. And then he went away.

The match today was, I am afraid, about as unsatisfying as the one that Warwickshire lost two years ago. But there were no dramas on the upper balcony.

Suddenly remembered at Lords this morning that I forgot to wear my Primary Club tie last Saturday. The Primary Club, as most keen cricket lovers will know, is an excellent organisation designed to raise money for blind children. Any cricketer who has ever been dismissed first ball in any class of cricket is entitled to join. Last year, as part of the launch celebrations for *Thomas Winsden's Cricketing Almanack,* my publisher helped to organise a special cricket match to raise funds for the club. As a result I was honoured to be made a life member. One of the rules is that the club tie should be worn on the Saturday of every Test Match. I think it is a splendidly English tradition.

All this reminds me that I recently heard that a publisher is bringing out an illustrated guide to cricket ties. It's bound to be an absolute winner! There cannot be too much wrong with a world in which there is a market for a book filled with nothing but pictures of cricket club ties.

Sunday 22nd July

I tried out my lob bowling theories today. I am not quite sure what went wrong but I suppose that the problem was that although I mastered line quite quickly, length eluded me.

Three deliveries in my first over landed on the pitch in front of the batsman and stopped quite dead. The batsman, quite unsportingly, insisted on taking a free hit at the ball on each occasion.

The first over cost us fourteen runs and the captain then took me off

Monday 23rd July

I was driving from Bristol to Leamington Spa today when I found myself scorching past a small, very pleasant looking cricket ground where two teams in white were engaged in battle. Suddenly realising that I really was not in much of a hurry after all I slowed down, stopped, turned round and went back to watch a few overs of their game.

I found it very depressing.

The players were probably about nine or ten years old. They should have been having fun, enjoying themselves, belting the ball around, and getting an hour or two's respite from the worries of growing up in a heavily pressured world.

They looked as miserable as if they were engrossed in a particularly tedious Latin lesson, or as if they were up to their eyes in algebraic equations. They looked smart and were, to a boy, neatly turned out. But they were not enjoying themselves.

Their teacher, a tart young man who was combining the roles of coach and umpire, was sharp tongued and quite remarkably aggressive. He seemed averse to praise, preferring instead to complain, condemn and sneer. When a bowler delivered a ball that was not on a good length he would castigate the unfortunate child as though he had just been responsible for the destruction of some priceless ornament. When a wicket fell he never congratulated the bowler or fielder responsible but always admonished the batsman for playing a careless or irresponsible shot.

I soon found myself feeling as depressed as the boy cricketers looked.

Those young school boys will grow up to hate cricket as much as they hate Shakespeare, trigonometry and compulsory press ups in the school gymnasium. That young school master will have successfully taught his young players to hate and despise a game that could give them a lifetime of pleasure.

You cannot instil cricket genius into a wayward sportsman by shouting at him. You cannot turn a uninterested player into a great player by screaming abuse at him. You cannot turn an incompetent batsman or bowler into a Test class player by using indiscriminate sarcasm.

Tuesday 24th July

Looking through last year's *Wisden's* I noticed that the year's county champions, Essex, lost no fewer than five first class matches. That means that they lost more matches than any other side down to 9th place in the championship table.

This supports a theory I have had for some time: that when playing in any sort of league table where there are points awarded to sides which win but no points deducted for sides which lose, it is much better to take chances and go for wins than it is to play safe. The county captain prepared to take risks, make courageous declarations and go for the runs whenever possible (such as Essex's Keith Fletcher) will certainly end up on the losing side a few times. But he will at least give his side a chance of winning. The county captain who is terrified of losing and. who hardly ever takes risks will be able to minimise his chances of losing. But he will end up with a lot of dull, drawn games to his credit.

As far as spectators are concerned the good news on all this is that the captains who offer cricket watchers the best bargain — good, exciting cricket — are most likely to end up with the rewards that accompany sustained success.

Wednesday 25th July
What a splendid day's cricket it was at Edgbaston today. It is not often that one can watch Warwickshire score over 400 runs in a single day.

I do not know what the players think of it but I do wholeheartedly approve of the new rule which stipulates that at least 117 overs a day must be bowled for the first two days of a county championship match. It will be interesting to see whether or not this new rule has any influence on the number of matches that end in a definite result.

Thursday 26th July
Have you noticed how newspapers are always much more interesting when they are old and you come across them by accident? Stories that you would not give a second glance to on the date of publication suddenly become quite fascinating when you find them wrapped around a packet of fish and chips. Newspapers that you would never dream of buying or reading provide compulsive entertainment when you find them lining forgotten drawers or tucked away in the car boot.

Today, while attempting to clean out the garden shed I came across a couple of pages from one of the quality Sunday newspapers. My eye was caught by a major feature written by former England captain and perennial fast bowler, Bob Willis.

Willis, I read, complains that the reason why there is such a dearth of fast bowlers in England is that all our youngsters are having the pace coached out of them. His argument is that schoolboy bowlers are constantly encouraged to make sure that they bowl a good line and length and that they are being told to concentrate on these two factors rather than on speed. The result is, he argues, that they end up bowling pleasant, neat, reliable medium pace; the sort of bowling that is probably the most effective for the average sort of bowler playing against the average sort of batsman but which is woefully ineffective against top class batsmen in Test Match cricket.

I must say I found this an extremely logical and acceptable argument, and I suspect that it probably applies to other departments of the game as well. Modern coaches seem obsessed with training youngsters to do things 'properly' and are wildly enthusiastic about ensuring that everything is done according to the book, (the book usually being the *MCC Coaching Manual.*) This attitude undoubtedly works well at school and club level but will inevitably damage the prospects of our ever managing to produce cricketers of really original talent; cricketers who can change the course of an innings and win a match by themselves. There have been text book cricketers who have been successful of course. Barry Richards and Tom Graveney are two names that spring to mind. But a convincingly high proportion of the very best cricketers do things that coaches would not approve of. I wonder how many coaches would have liked the young Botham to bat a little more carefully? I wonder how many coaches would approve of a young Jeff

Thomson or, indeed, a young Bob Willis? I wonder how many of the West Indians (a side full of truly natural talent) would have been turned into contemptibly ordinary club cricketers?

I can just see some earnest school master explaining to Gordon Greenidge just why he would have to change his batting stance if he ever wanted to succeed as a cricketer.

Friday 27th July

Another absolutely marvellous day's cricket at Edgbaston where Warwickshire managed to beat Hampshire by a whisker — taking the final Hampshire wicket with the penultimate ball of the match. Thrilling stuff that once again proves that when it is exciting, three-day cricket beats anything that the one-day competitions can offer.

There were some interesting moments early on in the day when Hampshire were waiting for Warwickshire to declare. One of the handful of spectators present called across to Trevor Jesty, acting Hampshire captain, suggesting that he gave opening batsman Chris Smith a bowl. The spectator's undisguised aim was clearly to help speed up the Warwickshire declaration. Much to everyone's delight Jesty responded by promising to give Smith an over and Smith surprised by quickly taking two wickets. One of the wickets he captured incidentally, was young Dyer who looked set to make his first championship century at the time. I have seen many players — Humpage, Smith, Ferreira and Lloyd, for example — get their maiden centuries over the years. It's always a rather warming experience. So that was slightly frustrating (though probably not as frustrating as it was for Dyer himself).'

The other sad moment of the day concerned that indomitable veteran Denis Amiss, who was left stranded on 98 not out when Norman Gifford finally declared the Warwickshire innings closed. Ferreira nearly got the great man run out trying to give him his chance to complete his eighty-ninth century. But it was not to be. It was the Hampshire captain, Jesty, who fielded the final ball of the Warwickshire innings and he looked almost apologetic as he did so, keeping Amiss from making his century of centuries. I hear that Amiss has a testimonial next year with Warwickshire and it would be splendid if he could reach that major milestone during what will almost certainly be a year of grateful celebrations. The Warwickshire supporters are full of affection for Amiss (in contrast, I am afraid, to their feelings for Bob Willis, whose departure will be welcomed by some members who feel that he has given too little to the club during his stay at Edgbaston).

Incidentally, I was rather distressed to notice during this match that the Hampshire players have got what looks desperately like an advertising slogan sewn onto their sweaters in the spot usually reserved for the county insignia. I have never noticed this before but it does look rather odd. I can still remember when John Snow got into dreadful trouble for allegedly wearing a minute advertising slogan on the back of his boot or somewhere equally obscure. You would have needed an astronomer's telescope to find out what it was that Snow was advertising. The Hampshire advertisements, if that is what they are, are easier to read but just as confusing. Why should a team of cricketers be advertising high explosives?

Saturday 28th July

I spent the morning busily occupied with my pocket calculator. Last year two hundred and four first class cricket matches were played in the Schweppes County Championship. A meagre ninety-nine matches ended with a definite result. That means that more than half of the matches played were drawn.

This year there have been one hundred and twenty-nine matches so far and of those sixty have ended in a definite result. That means that, once again, more than half of the matches played have been drawn.

I had rather hoped to be able to show that the new rules about minimum over rates had affected the number of first class matches ending with wins.

Pity.

Sunday 29th July
I have already commented on the fact that most of the people who do the catering at cricket grounds clearly still believe in pies, pasties and scotch eggs rather than nut cutlets, cottage cheese and whole bran biscuits.

Something else struck me today: is it not rather splendid that at cricket grounds the lavatories are still equipped with towel dispensers rather than those unspeakably inefficient hot air machines that never, ever work?

Monday 30th July
Modern railway stations may be convenient, dry and easy to maintain but they have none of the glamour and excitement of the Victorian railway stations built by our ancestors. Take the train from Coventry to Euston and you do not really get any genuine sense of *travelling*, do you? Those stations, undoubtedly designed by the same sort of empty suits who favour high-rise office blocks and ticky-tack box homes laid

out on neat estates, are uncompromisingly functional and avowedly unromantic.

Travel from Nottingham to St Pancras, however, and you really know that you are travelling. Both stations are still quite splendidly and defiantly archaic. You can almost hear the sound of the old steam trains chugging from the north of England, and the air somehow still seems thick with left-over smoke. Down at St Pancras, it is quite possible to imagine that the two gentlemen hurrying across towards the far platform are Sherlock Holmes and the faithful Watson, off on some errand of mercy. While the young gentleman with the cricket bag is undoubtedly Raffles setting off to play in a country house team and to relieve the owner of a few thousand pounds worth of unwanted jewellery.

But it was not Raffles today. It was Gilbert Johnson, a dear friend of mine whom I have known for years. We used to work together down at Southlands Hospital in Shoreham when dreams were still possible and one could still believe that Ted Dexter would come out of retirement to bring danger, sparkle and style back to Test cricket.

I had just arrived at St Pancras and Gilbert was early for his train and so we both had twenty minutes to spend in the station buffet drinking British Rail's sad apology for coffee. Gilbert, I knew, was captain of a club side in Wiltshire. When I asked how the club was doing Gilbert became very excited. He told me that he had high hopes and that a new acquisition he had just signed up seemed likely to add a new dimension to the club's future.

'He's going to revolutionise the club,' Gilbert told me proudly. 'There'll really be some changes during the next twelve months. It's the most important thing I've done for the club.'

'Batsman is he?' I asked.

'Not exactly,' Gilbert said. 'He's not really much of a batsman. Probably go in number ten or eleven.'

'Bowler then,' I said. 'Demon fast or unplayable googlies?'

'More gentle slow medium pace,' Gilbert answered, half apologetically. 'I expect I'll put him on as third change bowler if the pitch isn't taking spin.

'He's not a wicket-keeper then?'

'Ah, no. Fielding is his weak point I suspect.' Gilbert told me. 'I think I'll probably let him specialise at fine leg or third man. We'll be able to hide him down there.'

'Hang on a minute,' I said eventually 'Let me get this straight. This new chap of yours isn't much of a batsman and he doesn't bowl much and he's such a fearful liability in the field that you're going to have to hide him down in the country.'

Gilbert looked doubtful for a moment before admitting that I had summed things up fairly accurately.

'I know this is probably a pretty stupid question,' I confessed, 'but why are you so excited about him then?'

'He owns a sports outfitters and we're getting thirty percent off all our gear,' Gilbert explained.

Wednesday 1st August

Occasionally, one-day matches that look as though they should be exciting turn out to be disappointing. Today's quarter-final between Warwickshire and Surrey in the NatWest Trophy was one of those matches.

After a slightly uncertain start Warwickshire amassed an impressive total of 305 for the: loss of only five wickets. At that point there was still a chance that we would be in for a real thriller of a match. But within the first half a dozen overs of the Surrey innings the outcome of the match was settled. Surrey had lost three wickets for seventeen runs.

Once the chasing side loses that many quick wickets their chances of success plummet sharply. They cannot take any chances because if more wickets are lost they will not have enough batting capital to last them through the final hour of the match. And with over three hundred runs to score in order to win, the chasing side cannot afford to take things gently. If the remaining batsmen try to settle in and score slowly they will soon get behind the clock and find themselves chasing a quite impossible target.

That, as I say, is what happened to Surrey and the match turned out to be something of a disappointment.

Wins can sometimes be far less exciting than draws.

The Warwickshire total was built up by the three batsmen: K D Smith who scored 74, Denis Amiss, who picked up 73 and Alvin Kalicharran who scored 101. The adjudicator gave Alvin Kalicharran the Man of the Match Award, following the unofficial tradition that the batsman on the winning, side who scores the most runs will get the award. However, although Kalicharran's innings was important and good to watch I really did not think that Alvin was the Man of the Match. I would have given the medal, tie and cheque to Smith. He, after all, opened the innings, provided some stability when two quick wickets gave Surrey hope of a breakthrough and a low total to chase, and accelerated as soon as it became clear that Warwickshire were out of real trouble.

Smith's was an extremely well-balanced innings and one that really helped Warwickshire move into a match winning position. Since Smith himself was making his first appearance in the side for some time, and was undoubtedly anxious to make a good impression in order to retain his place, the innings he played was all the more remarkable.

Thursday 2nd August
There has recently been a tremendous amount of fuss about the Bodyline series of 1932-3. I suppose most of it is just left over from the 50th-anniversary celebrations.

This evening I watched an excellent documentary which included some tremendous footage of Jardine, Larwood, Allen and Wyatt. The one thing that struck me about it all was the extent of the difference between amateurs (exemplified by the chinless Jardine) and the professionals (such as the enigmatic Larwood, who manages to give the impression of being humble and self-effacing while at the same time making it clear that he is also stubborn and immensely proud).

It is difficult to believe that such huge differences existed a mere half-century ago.

The film also included a brief appearance by that fossilised cricket commentator E W Swanton. I had forgotten just how boring the *Daily Telegraph* used to be when Swanton's deathly-dull prose filled the cricket pages.

Friday 3rd August.
I spent some time this morning chatting to two cricket enthusiasts who work for a publishing house in London. They both argued ferociously that the England

selectors should abandon all their older players and go for youth.

'We've lost this series,' one pointed out, 'We should be trying to build a new side for the future.'

I disagreed with this theory for two reasons.

First, I do not think any Test Match should be abandoned as 'lost' or regarded as 'unimportant'. The country's selectors owe it to the team, the opposition, the fans and, indeed, to history to pick the team that is most likely to win the match.

Second, I think we have become far too obsessed with trying to find new 'young' players. We have become so obsessed with the miracle of youth that we have taken to disregarding and discarding skilful, reliable cricketers of the highest calibre just because they are only likely to be able to play for another few seasons. We have, I suspect, also become over anxious to pick young, agile players who will be able to sparkle on the field. Good fielding is of course, extremely important. Quick fielders can save runs and help win matches. But there is not much point in picking youngsters who can field well if they are not worth their places as batsmen or bowlers.

My own feeling is that one of the main reasons why we are currently trailing the West Indians 4–0 in this Test series is that our team contains too many inexperienced players. Look at the ages of the players in the last Test Match, for example and you will perhaps see what I mean:

Fowler 27, Broad 26, Terry 25, Gower 27, Lamb 30, Botham 29, Downton 27, Cook 28, Allott 27, Cowans 23, Pocock 37.

Only two members of the team are thirty years of age or over. And the average age of the whole team is just over twenty-seven.

Now compare the ages of the England players with the ages of the West Indian players. (Remembering too that Pat Pocock, the veteran of the England team, can hardly be described as an experienced Test player. He has not played Test cricket at all for eight years.) Their ages are:

Greenidge 33, Haynes 28, Richards 32, Gomes 31, Lloyd 39, Dujon 28, Holding 30, Baptiste 24, Harper 21, Davis 26, Garner 31.

No less than six of the West Indians are thirty years of age or over and the average age of the side is twenty-nine.

This age difference may be small but it is, I suspect, significant. If you look back through old copies of Wisden you will see that the great cricket teams of the past invariably had an average age of around twenty-nine. I picked out two sides purely at random and then checked out the ages of the players concerned. First, there is the England side which beat New Zealand at Lords in June 1958. I think you will agree that it is a powerful team. Their ages were:

P E Richardson 26, M J K Smith 25, T W Graveney 31, P B H May 28, M C Cowdrey 25, T E Bailey 34, T G Evans 37, G A R Lock 28, F S Trueman 27, J C Laker 36, P J Loader 28.

In that side there are four players over the age of thirty and the average age is over twenty-nine. Now take a look at the ages of the players in the Bodyline series. This is the team that beat Australia at Sydney in December 1932.

H Sutcliffe 38, R E S Wyatt 31, W R Hammond 29, Nawab of Pataudi 22, M Leyland 32, D R Jardine 32, H Verity 27, G O B Allen 30, L E G Ames 27, H Larwood 28, W Voce 23.

Again, there are five players over the age of thirty and the average age is twenty-nine.

I feel that any successful Test side needs a balance of experience and youth, of agility and wisdom, of promise and proven worth. The England selectors have gone overboard for youth with the result that at several times during this series there have been new and relatively untried batsmen at the crease.

Meanwhile, we have a number of experienced, well qualified Test class cricketers still playing in county cricket.

I think it is time the selectors began to think about the balance of the side they pick. I know that many of our most experienced players (Gooch, Boycott and Amiss) have been banned but there are others available and performing well enough to play a valuable part in the England side for a season or two to come.

Saturday 4th August

A mixture of rain and bad light meant that the only first class cricket played anywhere in England today was at Worcester where, although the start of play was delayed due to overnight rain, the weather was warm, sunny and bright enough for cricket watching.

With Nottinghamshire the visitors, I parked well away from the firing line of the batsmen — few modern cricketers hit the ball as hard or as far as Richard Hadlee. And within an horn: or two of the start Hadlee was indeed at the crease, partnered by his captain Clive Rice. At that point it was difficult to remember that this was Worcestershire playing Nottinghamshire in the Brittannic Assurance County Championship, since at one stage the Worcester attack consisted of Kapil Dev Kikhanj (born Chadigarh,

India) and Dipak Narshibhai Patel (born Nairobi, Kenya).

An Indian and a Kenyan bowling to a South African and New Zealander and we have the nerve to call it our domestic county championship!

The presence of at least two world class fast bowlers on the ground seemed to highlight the fact that umpires really do not apply any logic or commonsense to their thinking when they decide whether or not play should be allowed.

Richard Hadlee is undoubtedly one of the world's fastest bowlers at the moment. He is probably the fastest white bowler anywhere. Kapil Dev is widely regarded as the fastest bowler that India has ever produced. Is it not odd, therefore, that umpires should consider it reasonable to unleash bowlers of such tremendous pace on ordinary county batsmen, even though conditions are less than perfect, while they will steadfastly refuse to allow Test Match batsmen (theoretically the cream of the batting profession) to be exposed to fast bowling in anything other than perfect conditions? If Richard Hadlee can be a danger to England's opening batsmen, surely he can be an even greater danger to Worcestershire's opening batsmen? And, conversely, if Worcestershire's opening batsmen can safely cope with Richard Hadlee in less than perfect conditions, why do Test class opening batsmen have to be protected?

I do not know the answer to this question but I do suspect that the difference is that Test Match umpires are encouraged to take themselves and their duties far too seriously. And perhaps there is, too, the factor that the players at Test Match level, being highly paid, are conscious of the risk of injury and determined to avoid any chance of being put out of the game for a few weeks with a bruise or broken bone.

The pitch and outfield at Worcester today were damp enough for Mike Vockins, the soft-spoken club secretary, whose voice it is that broadcasts messages during the luncheon and tea intervals at Worcester, to ask young cricketers not to play on the grass during the intervals. I cannot remember the last time they instituted such a ban at Worcester.

The ban today led to a sad and rather sorry little confrontation behind the stand nearest to the main scoreboard. There is a decent sized patch of tarmacadamed roadway there and Sue, Neil and I (together with various other impromptu players who joined in as we played) were having a little gentle practice with a bat and an old tennis ball. Everyone who passed by smiled, and made a friendly comment or two, except for one sour looking fellow in a blue blazer who stopped and admonished Sue quite severely. Tediously, he warned her of the dangers of playing cricket in a public place and ended his lengthy admonishment with the immortal phrase 'I'm on the committee you know.'

Why, oh why, I wonder are there so many dull and boring fellows on cricket committees? Perhaps the rest of us should consider ourselves partly responsible for their status because it is, after all, our own indolence which puts them there. Perhaps these overly dull men obtain their positions of authority simply because they are the only cricket lovers who have both the time to spare to sit on committees and the inclination to do so.

They fit, these men, into what I shall call the Retired Major Syndrome. They are men who once had a position of minor authority — as army majors, hospital administrators, bank officials, police superintendents and so on — and having taken early retirement they need something to fill their days and satisfy their continuing need for superficial authority.

They ease onto our county cricket committee by default rather than by popular choice — their index-linked pensions give them the independence and the time to dedicate themselves to what they think of as 'good works'. You can see them at any county ground lounging in the committee rooms in overstuffed leather armchairs or sitting out on the balcony on slatted wooden benches. They wear blazers, grey flannels and club ties, they sport small toothbrush moustaches and their greying hair is combed straight back and trimmed to regulation army length. They are used to subservient behaviour from those around them and they treat the rest of the world with disdain and contempt; they are ignorant, arrogant and entirely worthless.

Sunday 5th August

While driving with my son Neil to a John Player League match I passed a van with *Winalot* printed on the side of it Neil suggested that the England cricket team should be given supplies of this no doubt nutritious food for hounds.

Incidentally, still musing about the Man of the Match selection at the NatWest match at Edgbaston the other day, I had a thought.

Would it not be possible for the crowd at one-day matches to select the Man of the Match ? On the back of each ticket or scorecard there could be a voting form. Then, at the end of the match spectators could put their voting form into a series of ballot boxes around the ground. It would not take much organisation and it would not take much counting either. (The cost would, probably be no more than the cost of bringing in an ex-England player to do the job.) The result could then be made available to the daily newspapers so that it could be printed in the next day's editions.

There could, perhaps, even be a record of the number of votes cast for each player.

Monday 6th August

I wonder how many indoor 'cricket' games there are?

When I was small I used to play the game with nothing more than a single dice. I would write out two favourite teams, and throw the dice to see which batted first. Then I would divide my teams into three segments. First, there would be the top line batsmen, then there would be the middle order batsmen and finally there would be the tail enders. Then I would start the game; choosing a bowler from the fielding side and keeping score in just the same way as any club cricket scorer does.

If the dice came up with a one, two, three, four or six then the batsman would have that score added to his total. If the dice came up with a five that would be considered an appeal, and I would throw the dice again. If the second throw produced a five then the batsman would be given out. To find out how the batsman had been out I would throw the dice a third time: a one indicated a clean bowled dismissal, a two indicated an LBW decision, a three indicated a catch, a four a run out, a five a stumped and a six a caught and bowled.

For middle order batsmen I changed the rules a little. They could be given out if the second throw produced a five or a six. And for a tail ender an appeal would result in a definite dismissal if a second throw produced a four, five, or six.

That simple dice game was one of my favourite pastimes for several reasons. First and foremost, it was extremely portable. All you needed was one dice, a piece of paper and a pencil. It was also quite suitable for playing at all sorts of odd moments — you could carry on with a match for days if necessary. You could play it by yourself too — vitally important for a schoolboy. Finally, it did tend to produce a fairly realistic sort of scoring pattern, with leading batsmen usually (but not always) getting the highest scores.

There were also games that used playing cards in a similar sort of way. For example, there was one game that used a chart to decide just what each pair of drawn cards meant. You would read off the colour and suit of each card and find out whether your batsman had blocked, scored or been dismissed.

And there was a game that used a little metal spinner with six sides. On each side of the spinner there were two sets of instructions. If on the first spin an appeal was made by the bowler then the second spin would show the consequence of that appeal. This was really very much the same sort of game as the one I have already described as suitable for a single dice.

These days cricket games are more sophisticated, although I do not think they are any more enjoyable. There are, for example, games involving specially printed cards and complicated rules which take a good deal of reading and understanding. And there is the Subuteo form of cricket in which players bowl and bat with tiny plastic figures and a miniature red ball. The only problem with all these games is that they require at least two players.

Now that I am older, I have become enamoured of two slightly more esoteric cricket games.

In the first, the aim is to think of situations not covered by the laws of cricket — or situations where the interpretation of the law might lead to a little discussion and controversy. So, for example, what happens if two batsmen collide in the middle of the pitch, equidistant from the two wickets and one is then run out? Which batsman is officially given 'out'?

The second is much more fun and involves creating imaginary cricket teams. One can try and pick a team of one-eyed batsmen to play a team of bowlers all more than six-feet tall. Or a team of players who bat in funny coloured pads versus a team of players who bat and field in oddly shaped headgear. This game can easily get out of hand when one starts picking teams which contain historical figures or characters out of fiction.

Here, for example, are two of my favourite imaginary teams:

The Imaginables
A team of heroic cricket players taken from fiction.

Falstaff, Hamlet, David Copperfield, Sherlock Holmes, Dr Watson, Captain Scott, Robinson Crusoe, Father Brown, Robin Hood, The Scarlet Pimpernel, Launcelot of the Lake.

The Historical
A team of cricket players taken from history.

King Charles I, W Wordsworth, Marco Polo, Julius Caesar, Idi Amin, Captain Bligh, Rasputin, Atilla the Hun, Tomas de Torquemada, Niccolo Machiavelli, Confucius.

Umpires: Judge Jeffries and Pontius Pilot.
Scorers: Jimmy 'the cricket bag' Morello and A. Einstein.

Tuesday 7th August

Sue and I met David Foster of Central Television today. David is mad keen on cricket and about to fly off to Spain to film holiday makers playing beach cricket with Spanish locals. (Television companies, like newspapers, tend to favour light stories during the month of August.) Before he rushed off to collect his pesetas he asked what had happened to last winter's Cricket Match on Ice. He, like most of my friends, had been invited to play in a Thomas Winsden out of season spectacular but unfortunately, due to a general lack of ice, the match had never materialised. (We had got fairly close to it once when a lake down near Bath very nearly froze over but a couple of warm days soon put paid to that expectation.)

Anyway, although it is rather depressing to think of winter while there are still a few weeks left of the cricket season, we did decide to go ahead with a match again this winter. I am not quite sure how we will get the stumps into the ice, or how the bowlers will manage to get any sort of grip when they run up to the wicket, but those are simple practical problems which I am sure we will be able to solve. The one factor we cannot control is the availability, of a suitable amount of ice.

That is something we will have to leave to the Great Groundsman in the Sky.

Wednesday 8th August

So David Gower, the curly haired boy wonder of English cricket, is to captain the touring team to India this winter.

I have always been an enthusiastic supporter of David Gower, the batsman. I remember watching his first stroke in Test cricket (he hooked a short pitched ball for four) and the immaculate double century that marked his early entry to international cricket. But I cannot help wondering whether or not Gower is the right man to be captaining England.

My main reservation is that he is too young and too inexperienced to take on the captaincy. He is twenty-seven now. Compare his age with the ages at which some of the most successful captains took on the responsibility and you will see that Gower is still remarkably young for such authority. Most of the successful Test captains have been at least thirty years of age before becoming captain. (There are exceptions such as Peter May, but exceptions they certainly are.)

Without having had much experience of captaining a county side Gower must surely be at a tremendous disadvantage when struggling to mastermind his national side's success in the cauldron of a Test arena. He is too young and too inexperienced, and the pressure of coping with the captaincy must surely have an adverse effect on his own batting skills. We can ill-afford to squander those much needed skills in the way that we temporarily squandered Botham's immense skills as an all-rounder by making him captain far too early on in his career. The idea of Gower captaining England is not as outrageous as the idea of Botham captaining England, but I would like to see Gower given a chance to win some honours with Leicestershire first of all.

Of course if Gower does not captain England then the selectors have a problem. The is no one else in the current England side who could possibly do the job.

Personally, I would like to see Keith Fletcher brought in to the side. He would not only bring experience and strength to the batting line up, he would also give us one of the best and most thoughtful captains currently available anywhere in the world. Sadly, I do not think the selectors will choose Fletcher, so perhaps they should carefully consider appointing a non-playing captain to look after the side, to provide general advice and leadership and to give the playing captain tactical instructions.

For that job there is no one better equipped than Mike Brearley — the one man who seems able to push players to the peak of their ability. Failing that, there is also Ray Illingworth — another experienced and successful ex-captain. Such a non-playing captain would, I suppose, fulfil the sort of role traditionally taken by a football team manager. Several first class English counties already have team managers and in that type of cricket the idea seems to work extremely well.

With a non-playing captain to advise him and take some of the pressure from him, David Gower *would* possibly be able to cope.

Without such support I think that he will continue to have problems.

Thursday 9th August

It was marvellous to see England doing so well at the Oval today, although I have to be honest and admit that I never really expected to see the West Indians dismissed for under 200. Even when they had lost seven wickets for under 100 I half expected to see a couple of their late order batsmen put together a mammoth score. The way the West Indians have been batting this summer one could almost believe that they have had a run-scoring rota system. Not until the last wicket fell did I really believe that England .was capable of controlling such a powerful line up of batting talent.

The best of the English bowlers was, once again, Ian Botham who took five wickets in an innings for the twenty-third time and who, during the day, took his 300th wicket for England. Botham is fearless and unpredictable: qualities which make him one of the most dangerous English cricketers of all time. Not since Ted Dexter's glorious days has there been an English batsman capable of tearing apart the best attacks in the world. Not since Fred Trueman has England had a bowler capable of destroying any opposition.

Botham as a batsman may not have much in the way of a defence and his bowling may often be expensive, but he is that rare cricketer: a potential match winner. And he is without a doubt one of the greatest all-rounders the world of cricket has ever seen. He will take his place in the history books alongside W G Grace, Garfield Sobers and Keith Miller.

What greater tribute can there be?

While Botham stamped his individual mark on yet another Test Match, young Ellison, one of the new caps in the England side, began what looks like being a long career as the great man's understudy. To me Ellison seems a not dissimilar cricketer to Hampshire's Trevor Jesty, but despite that there must be a few county cricketers around the country who felt a little peeved to see the young man from Kent acquiring an England cap with such a modest cricketing career behind him.

Despite a lack of proven experience however, Ellison seems to have what it takes to survive at Test Match level and I suspect that he has a wealth of experience ahead of him. You can have all the cricketing skills in the world but if you have neither luck nor temperament those skills will be useless. England has had a number of 'almost' players over the last few years and the selectors have often persevered with them to a point where even the players themselves must have felt embarrassed; Gatting is the prime example of a cricketer rising beyond his skills, unable to match his undoubted prowess with the bat with the necessary mental powers.

On the other hand there are players such as Fowler who have modest match skills but a tremendous temperament for big match situations. Fowler is not a great batsman but he has courage, patience and luck. I am not yet convinced that Ellison has greatness in him but his appearance at the Oval today suggested that he may have some of those other essential qualities.

I just hope that the critics do not expect him to match Ian Botham's skills. No country can hope to have two cricketers with both luck and courage as well as genius.

Friday 10th August
There is news today about a new scheme designed to try to find a fresh supply of English fast bowlers. Sponsored by a brewery, a team of experts is planning to scour the country for athletic young men who can be turned into the Larwoods and Lillees and Lindwalls of the late 1980s.

Ted Dexter and Bob Willis are reported to be among the ex-cricketers involved in the scheme.

The argument put forward by the proponents of this new scheme is that it is perfectly possible to take a young man of eighteen or so and, provided that he is a natural athlete, supremely fit and extremely enthusiastic, turn him into a world class fast bowler. It is, I suppose, the cricketing equivalent of the Pygmalion story and Bob Willis seems destined to play the Professor Higgins role. Fast bowlers, say the scheme's supporters, do not need to be born or carefully nurtured; they can be hewn from raw flesh within twelve months or so.

The project has met with a fair amount of opposition. Much of it has come, predictably enough, from former cricketers, who have argued with some pride that bowling is a craft and that players must serve a long, thoughtful apprenticeship if they expect to reach the highest levels of the game.

There have, however, been many expert observers ready to agree that the scheme may offer English cricket new hope for the future. These observers have argued that in the world of athletics it is not at all unusual for coaches in some disciplines to find and train new recruits in a relatively short space of time. In some of the field events (the javelin, the shot put, the hammer and the discus, for example) fit young men and women have been turned into top class performers in the space of a few months.

It is true, they agree, that no one could produce a top class spin bowler in twelve months or create an international class batsman with a high intensity coaching course, but fast bowling is something quite different and fast bowlers need pace more than anything else. Fast bowlers, they claim, can be manufactured. It will be a fascinating experiment.

Saturday, 11th August
Today we drove up to Chatsworth in Derbyshire for a huge family picnic. There were relatives there from Devon, Kent and Wales as well as various parts of the Midlands and North of England. Although cold, gloomy and often isolated in winter, the countryside in this part of Derbyshire is, in summer, exquisitely English, with rolling hillsides, woodland glades, fast

flowing rivers and streams, and acres of sheep cropped parkland decorated and divided with neat dry stone walling.

We shared our luncheon baskets in a delightfully sheltered spot just outside the grounds of Chatsworth House. Above us ran a quiet country lane, hardly used even in summer. Below us a clean sparkling river wound its way between tree-studded banks. There were ducks on the river and sheep on the opposite bank. A bright sun shone down from a blue sky dotted with a handful of fluffy clouds. It is difficult not to think of everything in poetic terms when the surroundings are so perfect.

By the time we had emptied our picnic baskets and filled our stomachs, the meadow in which we were settled had become quite busy, with several other parties (mostly smaller than ours) opening their flasks, peeling hard boiled eggs, chopping up their tomatoes, shaking the water from their lettuce and opening up their cold meats, and pork pies. I watched all this with the comfortable half interest of a man who has eaten well and has nothing much to occupy his mind.

But my interest in what was going on around me quickly became more acute when I noticed that as they finished their picnics many of my neighbours started playing cricket. A few began paddling in the river (it was bright and fresh and there was not a bottle, plastic bag or old bedstead to be seen). One or two took out their newspapers. But, on the whole, men and women, young and old, children and grandparents, seemed determined to enjoy themselves by playing our national game. There were, within half an hour or so, no less than half a dozen separate games taking place. Men rolled up their sleeves, tossed back their thinning hair and imagined that they were Fred Trueman coming in to bowl or Sir Len Hutton about to take another hundred off the Australians. Grandfathers loosened their braces, took off their flat caps and cast aside their jackets. Mothers slipped off their shoes and darted about gaily, giggling a good deal at the incomprehensibility of it all. Even teenage girls and tiny tots took it all in good part.

Hardly any of them had proper cricket equipment, of course. There were, I suppose, no more than two bats between the lot of them. And there were no such things as stumps, bails, pads or cricket whites. Instead of cricket balls (uncomfortably hard and horribly expensive) they used tennis balls, usually old and battered.

For stumps they used anything that came to hand: a wire rubbish basket, a plastic water carrier, an up-ended briefcase that had presumably been used to transport sandwiches, a tree trunk and a pile of coats and jumpers. Those who had no proper cricket bats used tennis rackets, badminton rackets or pieces of rotten tree branches dragged from the river and stripped of loose bark and unnecessary branches. One enterprising team used a multi-coloured golfing umbrella, another used a tightly rolled copy of a women's magazine.

I greatly enjoyed watching these impromptu games where there was no concern about averages, prize money, bouncers or no-balls. There were good natured controversies about LBW decisions and some merry arguments about just where the boundary was situated, but the one thing that all these cricket matches had in common was that they were played entirely for fun. No one played who did not want to, no one played out of a sense of obligation and no one played with hope of any glory or subsequent approbation.

Watching them, I was reminded of the days when I worked as a general practitioner with another cricket-mad doctor and used to play impromptu games in our health centre after morning surgery. One of us would bat in the spaciousness of the waiting room while the other would use the long corridor for his run up. We would, use a rolled up copy of the *British Medical Journal* as a bat and a few pieces of scrap paper, firmly bundled together, as a ball. Our games used to become quite sophisticated, with pot plants and chairs designated as fielders and one of the receptionists instructed to act as wicket-keeper.

The older members of the MCC may look down their noses at this type of cricket, and it may not be quite what the modern architects of the game have in mind when they sit down to muse and pontificate about the future of the sport. But this type of gentle, unorganised cricket does have a place in the modern game. It was, after all, in much the same sort of way that the game originated several hundred years ago. They were playing cricket with such primitive props long, long before batting gloves and helmets and thigh pads were available.

And if I had to put money on any form of cricket lasting through the next few centuries it would be the type of cricket played with battered old tennis balls and rolled up magazines rather than the type played by highly paid professionals in huge sporting arenas.

Sunday 12th August

I do get slightly cross about the fact that although I have a parking pass for three county grounds I invariably have to arrive a good half an hour before a game starts in order to guarantee getting into the car park. At Edgbaston, for example, there is a huge park but the club sells so many car park passes that there are always members with tickets being turned away.

That seems to me to be rather immoral, on a par with that dreadful airline habit of selling more tickets than there are seats on the aeroplane.

I would be prepared to pay a higher subscription fee if it would guarantee me somewhere to park the car. Perhaps the Warwickshire Committee should think of offering two types of car park pass: 'Guaranteed' and 'If You're Lucky'.

Monday 13th August
At the Oval today the umpires seemed to spend an awful lot of time shouting at the crowd and getting them to keep quiet and still. Now I can quite understand how annoying it must be for a batsman if spectators sitting behind the bowler's arm are ill-mannered enough to keep moving around. Against any bowling attack that would be a dreadful nuisance against the fearsome West Indian bowling attack it is potentially lethal.

But I do think that the umpires have got rather carried away with it all in this match. Once or twice the umpires walked across to spectators sitting many yards away from the area around the sightscreen. Just why batsmen should be disrupted by movements so far away from the line of attack is something I do not understand.

Nor do I think that the umpires are entirely justified in complaining about the noise at cricket matches. I think spectators might be justified in complaining when the noise becomes outrageous, but why should the players be worried? And what on earth is the point of the umpires trying to get involved if the ground authorities are not interested in the problem? When noisy spectators are allowed to bring drums and trumpets onto cricket grounds the authorities can hardly be said to have taken any interest in subduing excessive enthusiasm.

It is not just at the Oval that spectators are getting told off a good deal these days. The other day, while watching a three-day match at Edgbaston, I saw an umpire shout at a spectator who was struggling to push the sightscreen into the required position. The umpire and one or two of the players were screaming instructions at the unfortunate fellow who really had no idea what was required of him. I have to say that although I was sitting some distance from the sightscreen I sympathised with the spectator: I could not work out what was wanted.

Then, suddenly and quite unexpectedly, the spectator decided that he had taken enough abuse. 'I'm doing you a favour,' he shouted. 'I paid to come in here. You move the bloody thing yourselves.' And with that he sat down.

A couple of fielders then had to run across and move the screen to the position where they wanted it.

I thought it was a splendid moment. Spectator power!

Tuesday 14th August•
It is the semi-finals of the Nat West Trophy tomorrow and I am not sure whether to go the Edgbaston to see how Warwickshire get on or drive down to Lords to watch Middlesex.

I do have to confess that as an MCC member I am torn about whether or not to keep my fingers crossed for Middlesex.

If Middlesex win then the pavilion at Lords will be crowded with Middlesex supporters on the day of the final. They will all be eager to watch their team from the best vantage point in England

If Middlesex fail to reach the final then the only people crowding into the pavilion will be MCC members eager to watch a good day's cricket.

In other words, if Middlesex win then the pavilion will be far more crowded than if they lose. As an out-of-town member who has difficulty in getting to Lords before ten in the morning I hope I can be forgiven for nurturing such a selfish thought.

On balance I think I will probably drive over to Edgbaston and see if Warwickshire can repeat their impressive performance against Surrey in the quarter-finals of this tournament.

Another glorious day for Chris Old today who has now become the first player to take ten wickets both for Yorkshire and against them in first class fixtures. He took his ten Yorkshire wickets in the match that was completed at Headingley today. He ended up with a match analysis of 11 for 99 runs.

Few bowlers can have ever enjoyed such sweet success.

Wednesday 15th August

Warwickshire do not seem to have much luck with the toss in one-day matches. Today's toss must have had a significant effect on the outcome of the match with Kent at Edgbaston. There was plenty of mist around during the morning session and the ball certainly seemed to be moving about considerably.

Once again Alvin Kallicharran was the outstanding Warwickshire player — with a tremendous innings of 86. The next highest scorer was Extras who put together 28!

The Warwickshire total was never really enough to enable them to win and Kent won easily by six wickets with a couple of overs to spare. In fact, I think that the apparently close margin of victory probably flatters Warwickshire. It seemed a fairly certain victory for Kent from the moment when Warwickshire had both openers, Amiss and Humpage, back in the pavilion with less than 100 runs on the scoreboard.

The batting and bowling averages make pretty fascinating reading today. It is good to see Denis Amiss right up there near the top of the averages. I do hope that we are going to see him recalled to the England side next year, when the stupid South African ban is over. Apart from Mike Gatting and Peter Denning (who has only been dismissed five times this season and who is, therefore, flattered by his position) the English batsmen in the top ten (Amiss, Gooch and Boycott) are all banned at the moment. Gooch, by the way, is still in the bowling averages. But the man who has really taken the averages by storm this summer is Richard Hadlee who, with 880 runs and 88 wickets to his name, seems set to complete the double. And what a double: his current batting average is 55 while his wickets have cost him a mere 14 runs apiece. The leading wicket taker in England is, almost predictably, the seemingly immortal John Lever. A less predictable name among the top few bowlers today is Terry Alderman — it is good to see that Alderman has recovered from that most unfortunate accident that put him out of the game for so long. His season with Kent should have prepared him for the next Australian tour of England. And all true cricket lovers must welcome that.

Thursday 16th August

A friend mine tells me that he was coming back from a business meeting recently when he drove past umpire Dickie Bird on a motorway. He says that Mr Bird was driving in the slow lane and although the weather was perfectly bright he had his headlights switched full on.

My friend, an enthusiastic cricket supporter, suggests that this anecdote is of some significance. He argues that if Mr Bird needs his headlights in broad daylight then it is hardly surprising that he cannot see well enough to justify there being any play when he is umpiring and the light is anything short of dazzling.

I do not believe he saw Dickie Bird at all.

But it is a nice story.

Saturday 18th August

Sue, Neil and I drove down to Camberley in Surrey for a cricket weekend with the Adventurers Club and Leaping Lord Thackelay's XI. The main match between the two sides is scheduled for tomorrow (I play for the Adventurers Club), but today we had an impromptu match on a local village green just outside Camberley. I tried out my lob bowling yet again but I still do not seem to have mastered the technique, I am not convinced, however, that lob bowling could not be re-introduced into professional cricket with some success. I shall continue to experiment with this technique during the winter months. Perhaps it will work well in our cricket match on ice.

The most important part of the day was the cricket club dinner held in the early evening. The main course was duck (what else is suitable for a cricket club dinner?) and the chef had turned fresh oranges into sorbet-filled cricket balls by dyeing them bright, cherry red. The restaurant where the dinner was held had provided two long dining tables for the teams and the place cards for the dinner had been very cleverly arranged as though the diners were fielders.

So, for example, at the top of the Adventurers Club table the president was sitting in a position marked Bowler. At the far end of the table, sitting in a position called Wicket-Keeper, was the club secretary.

On the president's right sat the club treasurer (sitting in the Mid-On position) while on his left sat the more experienced of the club's opening batsmen (sitting at Mid Off). On the Wicket-Keeper's right sat the other opening batsman (sitting at First Slip) while on the Wicket-Keeper's left sat the club's only leg break bowler (sitting at Backward Short Leg). The other places around the table were defined in a similar way with Second Slip, Third Slip, Gully, Backward Point, Point, Silly Mid Off and Short Extra Cover filling in the left hand side of the table. The right hand side of the table was occupied by Backward Short Leg, Short Leg, Forward Short Leg, Silly Mid On, and Mid Wicket.

I am told that the speeches made at the dinner were amusing.

I am afraid, however, that I cannot remember anything I heard. It must have been a splendid event.

Sunday 19th August

After my game for the Adventurers Club today the president, Sir Bertie Wheezer, said, that as a cricketer, he thought that I was an all-rounder. Before I could glory in this praise, however, he explained that he meant that I was equally bad at bowling, batting and fielding. I may never play again.

Monday 20th August

Cricket terminology is very strange, is it not?

Sue asked me today where the term 'gully' came from. I produced several half-hearted explanations but had to admit that I really did not know. Then she wanted to know where the term 'covers' had originated. Again,, I managed all sorts of spurious answers. But I could not think of an answer that I could swear was true.

'And why do they call it a batting crease?' she wanted to know. 'It sounds as though they fold the pitch up at the end of the day. '

That had me stumped.

'And why do you always refer to the chap with the bat as. the batsman while the follow who is bowling is a bowler. Why not call them batter or bowlsman? And why is it a fielder rather than a fieldsman?'

By that time I had completely run out of answers.

Wednesday 22nd August

So many of the England openers have been injured this season that a strange thought has occurred tome.

If an opening batsman is injured early on in the innings, has to leave the field of play to receive medical attention and only returns to the crease when the number eleven batsman is batting, can he be said to have carried his bat if he remains 'not out' when the innings ends?

Thursday 23rd August

I have always tried to visit Lords for the Thursday of a Test Match there. Friday is probably the best day for cricket watching (you can usually expect to see the end of one innings and the start of another) but Thursday is always a special day. And this, being the first Test match that Sri Lanka have played in this country means that today is a very special day indeed.

How many people can say they have watched an international side playing its first Test at the headquarters of cricket?

Friday 24th August
I happened to be in Bournemouth today and, finding myself with an unexpected hour to spare, I gave a taxi driver enough to buy himself a small home on the French Riviera to take me to the Hampshire ground.

I have always liked watching cricket near the sea. I do not know whether it is because the air is so exceptionally bracing or because the sight and sound of so many sea gulls bring back happy memories of seaside holidays and days of lazy pleasure. I did live on the south coast, once, at Shoreham, just a couple of miles along from Brighton, but although I thoroughly enjoyed the experience I was, in the end, quite glad to leave. The problem was that when you live by the sea you take it all for granted. All the excitement of a day trip to the coast disappears when you just have to wander a couple of miles down the road to see the breakers and buy a stick of rock.

The Hampshire ground was pretty empty when I got there and I found myself sharing most of one stand with an extremely earnest looking gentleman whose bald head was burnt to a dark brown colour by the sun. We were sitting some twenty or thirty yards apart, and to begin with I took no notice of him at all. He had a large notebook stretched out across his knees and seemed engrossed in it.

I had not been sitting there for more than fifteen minutes when I was awoken from my pleasant reverie by the sound of a sudden isolated burst of applause. I looked across and saw that the hairless spectator with whom I was sharing the stand had put down his pencil and was clapping enthusiastically. I thought little of it. I could not see any cause for such a dramatic expression of approval but I had been dozing a little and I was not sure if I had missed a well struck shot or a keenly flighted delivery.

It happened again after another ten minutes. Once more I could think of no explanation for the applause. And no one else on the ground was clapping. And then again after another quarter of an hour or so. So it went on. Four or five times in the next hour my companion suddenly shattered the silence with a fiercely appreciative round of applause. Curiosity aroused, I kept a very close eye on the balding enthusiast. When, after another thirty minutes or so, it was time for me to leave I made my way over to where he was sitting, hoping to have a word with him and find out just why he was clapping and just what I and the other spectators on the ground had been missing.

As you have undoubtedly guessed, by now (I had not guessed although I admit I should have done) the balding gentleman with the large notepad on his knees was an enthusiastic Amateur Statistician. He was applauding minor milestones in his club's history. The difference was, however (and this explains why the other spectators had missed these statistical milestones and failed to celebrate them with a little palmar oscillation) that the lone statistician was keeping track neither of the batsmen nor of the bowlers.

He told me that he had for many a year harboured an earnest wish to make his mark on cricket statistics but that the almanacs and cricket magazines all had their own resident experts. There was, he reasoned, no opportunity for a statistician who recorded all the usual statistics about wickets taken and runs scored.

And so he had decided to specialise in fielders and fielding. While he kept his records meticulously up to date, he told me that he kept records of every time a fielder stopped a ball, let a ball go through, caught a ball, dropped one and every other missed opportunity. With the aid of a complex system of handicapping which I did not entirely understand, he had worked out a way to measure the number of runs that each individual fielder had saved. He had averages only for his own home county but he could tell me which fielders had the best averages and which fielders were worth their places for the runs they had saved.

And the clapping that I had not been able to understand? Well, every time a fielder reached a small personal milestone (50 runs saved in an innings, 200 runs saved in a season or whatever) then he clapped.

I left Bournemouth confused and just a little wiser, and convinced that the statisticians will eventually take over the game completely. I was very impressed by my bald friend s dedication and singlemindedness. I wonder if the statistical gurus will ever follow his example. Heaven help us if they do. We will all have raw hands.

Saturday 25th August

Although it is invariably stodgy and filling (excellent qualities for cricket watching), the food at some county grounds does fall far short of decent catering standards.

The only thing that upsets me about Worcester, for example, is the fact that they do not sell good pies. It is a beautiful, friendly ground, but when are they going to offer their members and guests a decent pork pie?

Sunday 26th August

John Inchmore's benefit plans are continuing at quite a pace and I have just produced a feature for his benefit brochure. Although I shall do all I can to help him, and although I fork out for cricketers' benefits wherever and whenever they take place, I do think the time has come to reconsider the whole question of offering benefits and testimonials.

The system reeks of the old Soup Kitchen mentality. It cannot be particularly pleasant for a player to have to spend a year practically begging for money to put into his pension fund. Nor can it be much fun for players waiting to see whether or not their own committee is going to allow them a benefit.

I think it is time the system was abandoned and players were given not only an annual fee or salary but also some sort of investment programme, paid for by the club on their behalf This would mean that the longer a player stayed with a club, the bigger the sum of money he would obtain — so players would still be under some pressure to remain faithful to their clubs.

Those individuals who love organising raffles and dances could still do so — but instead of handing the money over to one player they would hand the money over to the playing staff's investment programme.

It would, I feel, be a much more civilised way of running things.

Monday 27th August

I spent the day chatting to a couple of cricket watching friends trying to define the Real Cricket Lover. We came up with this set of guidelines.

1. The Real Cricket Lover turns up at the county ground at eleven am whatever the weather may be.

2. Even if it is raining the Real Cricket Lover stays on the ground until the umpires have abandoned play for the day.
3. The Real Cricket Lover always stays for the end of a match, even if it is painfully obvious that the match is going to be a tedious draw.
4. Real Cricket Lovers carry their county membership cards with them everywhere they go.
5. Real Cricket Lovers never need to show their membership cards. The gatemen known them too well.
6. If they have motor cars, Real Cricket Lovers always carry pads, bat, gloves and a ball in them — just in case.
7. Real Cricket Lovers always stand up to applaud a good innings.
8. A Real Cricket Lover still uses linseed oil on his bat even if it is sealed and does not need oiling.
9. A Real Cricket Lover usually drinks beer, lager or shandy, occasionally drinks champagne, wine or gin but never drinks anything else.
10. Real Cricket Lovers enjoy one-day cricket but know it is not *really* cricket.
11. A Real Cricket Lover usually watches matches at two local grounds so that he can get a matching sun tan. (At the one ground he sits with the sun on his left. At the other ground he sits with the sun on his right.)
12. The Real Cricket Lover has a special bag into which to cram such cricket watching impedimenta as a waterproof coat, a vacuum flask, a plastic box for sandwiches or biscuits, a pencil with a rubber on the end and a small, pocket cricket annual.

Tuesday 28th August
Malcolm Mortimer, my friend who plays cricket in the Nottingham area, tells me that he has been having a

sizzling season both with the bat and with the ball. He has made up with his captain and is getting a regular bowl these days. He telephoned me today and asked whether I thought it was possible for a player who had not experienced county cricket to get an England cap. He said he was only asking for a friend and that he has rung me because of my association with the MCC.

I told him that I could not see why a player should not be allowed to play for England without having any county experience. Malcolm was clearly thrilled by this. He said he would get in touch with his friend straight away and give him the good news.

He then asked me whether I thought a chap would need to have typhoid and cholera injections to go to India and Pakistan.:

Richard Hadlee finally succeeded yesterday. The first man for seventeen years to complete the cricketing double of 1000 runs and 100 wickets. It was a tremendous achievement by a marvellous cricketer but it has left me with a nagging worry: just why are there no English cricketers around who look like repeating the achievement? Can we really blame the amount of one-day cricket that is played? Is the reduction in the number of first class matches really the only explanation?

Or are we just going through a particularly lean period in English cricket?

Wednesday 29th August
It has only just dawned on me that we were completely humiliated by the West Indians this summer. I had, I suppose, switched, off to a certain extent unwilling to acknowledge what was happening. But a five-nil thrashing is a pretty fearful indictment of English

cricket. I honestly cannot believe that the team the West Indians brought over is *that* good.

The only comfort is that it was not the Australians who beat us five—nil. Now that really would have been awful.

Somehow the Tests we play against the Australians seem so much more important than the Tests we play against other countries.

I would rather lose to the Falklands Islands than lose the Ashes at home by such a convincing margin.

Thursday 30th August
There is only one thing that annoys me more than hearing cricket commentators say 'Ah, well, cricket's a funny game you know', and that is hearing a cricket commentator describe a fielder as 'giving chase' when he runs after a ball that has been hit towards the boundary.

I suspect that this cumbersome phrase 'giving chase' has been picked up by commentators who have spent too much time talking to policemen. It is the sort of phrase the police love to. use when describing their exploits. Listen to a police constable give evidence in court and he will never say 'I chased the villain'; instead he will say 'I gave chase'.

Friday 31st August
Today I picked up an old copy of a daily newspaper and found a story about a man who has inherited a cricket pitch. What a glorious tale it is. A cricket loving chap called Jim Hews acquired the club and ground when his sixth cousin (a lady he had never even heard of) died and left him the lot in her will. Mr Hews' club is down in Somerset at a place called Brompton Ralph, a delightful little village hidden away in the wilds of

the West Country. Indeed, the story brought back many happy memories for me, because I once spent a marvellous Saturday afternoon there watching a local game.

The playing area is on a slope and at one point in the afternoon one of the fielders was completely out of sight. I can still remember my surprise at seeing this chap coming into sight as he rose up over the artificial horizon. It was like something out of *England Their England*. What a surprise it would be for a batsman to send a ball high into the air, way out of sight and then to see a fielder appear with the ball in his hand claiming a catch. Actually at Brompton Ralph it can get a little tricky hitting the ball into the air — there are one or two stray electricity cables crossing the pitch and an over-enthusiastic shot can easily become tangled with the National Grid.

The only other thing I can remember about this delightful cricket club is that the pitch is also on a slope. Several slopes to be precise. Playing there must be a bit like playing cricket in a saucer.

But, oh how I envy you Mr Hews. I would rather like to own my own cricket club and pitch.

Saturday 1st September

I have not written anything about the Test Match against the Sri Lankan team until today because I wanted to let my initial shock and dismay melt away before starting to hammer the typewriter keys.

Now that I feel calmer and cooler I feel better able to comment objectively on England's performance.

Never, in my thirty years of cricket watching, have I seen such a dismal and pitiful display by any representative side. Never before have I seen such laughably inept performances by players who think of themselves as among the best in the world. And never before have I seen such wimpish leadership. David Gower makes Mike Denness look potent by comparison.

Like most true cricket lovers I lost almost all interest in the game after the very first day. The interest I did retain was inspired simply by admiration for the Sri Lankan team's skill and determination. I thought they played magnificently. They certainly deserved to win. And if they had won then I would have stood up and cheered what could only have been a victory for the game of cricket.

There is talk in the newspapers today about Gatting and Tavare (captains of Middlesex and Kent in today's Nat West Trophy Final) being prospective vice-captains for the coming tour of India. I really cannot see how anyone can consider either of these two men worth a place in an England touring party.

Sunday 2nd September

Drove to Weston Super Mare to see some chums and spent most of the day playing cricket on the enormous sandy beach there. Beach cricket is a long established tradition among English holiday-makers and there cannot be many amateur players who have not bowled and batted on sandy wickets. Most beach cricket is fairly casual, of course, with pieces of driftwood being used as bats and rocks as wickets. Our match today was much better organised. One of my pals had brought three stumps, two bails and a bat, another had brought a couple of rather tattered old tennis balls.

We divided ourselves into a couple of teams and began just as the tide was turning, not realising how fast the tide rushes in.

The result was that whereas the side which fielded first had the luck to bowl on a fairly dry wicket, which took a tremendous amount of spin, the side which fielded last had the task of bowling on wet sand, with an inch or so of water spread across the wicket. I do not know whether you have ever tried playing cricket in an inch of water but if not then take my word for it: you cannot get the ball to bounce at all.

As a result, my team lost. We were, indeed, humiliated.

We are, however, reporting the pitch to Lords. It will be interesting to see what they have to say.

Monday 3rd September
Young Paul Smith of Warwickshire could go right to the top in professional cricket. He has opened both the batting and the bowling for the county and, although he still has a lot of faults, he does seem to have fire and determination in him. So many young players seem to bowl at medium pace and to bat with great caution that it is a pleasant surprise to find a youngster prepared to throw his heart and soul into the game. Of course he will get dismissed for nought occasionally and he will get thrashed around the ground a good deal. But I hope he does not settle down too much. He bats and bowls rather like a young Botham: full of raw energy and danger. At twenty, he is a cricketer to watch.

Tuesday 4th September
Played cricket again yesterday, but I do have to admit that I am basically a voyeur. Nothing gives me greater pleasure than watching cricketers run around getting sweaty. I like it best when they are working so hard that their brows glisten and their breath is slightly laboured.

I used to be much more of a participant. And not just at cricket. There was a time when I would spend my Friday evening oiling my bat, scraping the mud off my golf shoes and counting my maggots. I would spend hours rubbing the grass stains off my tennis balls and invest far more than I could afford in lenses and filters.

The truth came to me in a dash of light, quite suddenly and unexpectedly one summer a couple of seasons ago. I had spent three hot hours fielding at third man and was slowly making my way back to the pavilion when I happened to pass a pair of lazy good-for-nothings sitting in deck chairs, surrounded by crumpled beer cans. They had clearly spent the afternoon doing absolutely nothing useful but contribute to the profits of a major brewery.

As I limped wearily into the pavilion, where I knew there would be handfuls of slightly crumpled sandwiches sitting alongside an urn of almost undrinkable tea, I felt rather aggrieved. It did not seem fair. But then slowly the bitterness dissolved as I realised that I did not have to be a participant. I too could become a voyeur.

It was in some ways a difficult decision to make. Our society is a very participatory one. People tend to feel guilty if they are not doing something useful all the time. But I do not feel guilty anymore. I play occasionally, usually on beaches and in gardens, but I spend most of my summer watching other people play cricket.

The sad thing is, however, that even cricket watching is becoming a participatory sport. At one-day and Test matches it is not good enough these days to sit there quietly while the gentle thud of leather on willow reassures you that things are still happening. Today there are cups to be won, money to be fought for and teams to be supported. If you are a spectator you are expected to bang your beer cans together, jump up and down with joy every twenty seconds and put up with the banners and mindless chants that have become an accepted way of life for some cricket watchers.

I find all this worrying. How long will it be before the real cricket spectators are overrun by these lunatics? How long before the Woolly Jumpers are overrun by the Can Bangers?

Or will three-day cricket, the cricket I love best, remain safe from these modern intruders, too dull to merit their unwelcome attention?

Wednesday 5th September
Today I spoke to Darley Anderson, a publisher and cricket enthusiast. He told me that he had thoroughly enjoyed the series of Test Matches this summer. When I expressed some slight surprise at this he explained that half way through the season he had decided that England were not only going to lose but that they were not worth supporting. He had, therefore, switched allegiance and supported the West Indian team for the second half of the season. Apart from a moment or two of worry when the West Indians were dismissed for a paltry 190 in their first innings at the Oval, he had a delightful summer.

I told him that I thought there were probably plenty of other cricket enthusiasts who would wish that they had done likewise. But I also reminded him that the Australians are coming next year. And that no stout Englishman could even dream of supporting *them*.

Incidentally, that conversation with Darley Anderson reminded me of a momentous gaffe I made a few years ago. It was the last time the West Indians were here and for weeks before they arrived I was involved in the preparation of a book that needed some rather complicated editing and setting. These complications necessitated my spending an hour or so a day on the telephone to the publishers in London. While chatting to my editor there I found out that she shared my passion for cricket.

The crunch came when, the day after the West Indian team had landed, I laughingly suggested that we would be able to thrash them without too much difficulty. I made some uncomplimentary remarks about their team.

There was a horrible silence from the other end of the telephone and then the editor spoke.

'We haven't met, have we?' she reminded me in a unusually quiet voice.

I agreed that we had not.

'I'm West Indian,' she told me.

Thursday 6th September

I spent the day watching cricket at a ground that shall be nameless. The cricket was soothing but forgettable. There was, however, one memorable moment. The ladies' lavatory had been closed for alterations and a chalked sign on a large blackboard explained this fact to all unfortunate would-be customers. 'Temporarily shut for improvements.' read the sign. 'We apologise for the inconvenience.'

I thought it as fine a piece of official graffiti as I have seen for a long, long time.

Friday 7th September

I dreamt of Mr Hews last night. And his cricket club at Brompton Ralph. This morning I telephoned my mother and got her to check round all our relatives. I wanted to be absolutely sure that I do not have any sixth cousins hidden around the country who own cricket clubs.

Do you know, I think I would rather own my own cricket club than play for England.

Saturday 8th September

I travelled to Manchester today to play in a friendly game against a team which consists of a real mixture of local enthusiasts. They enjoy their cricket a great deal are captained by a remarkable fellow who has a sense of humour and lives in a terraced house called Dun Stumpin.

A few minutes before the match started, the captain of the opposing team came into our dressing room and asked us to try and let their number four batsman score one or two runs.

'It does not have to be anything too much,' said the captain quietly, 'but if you could let him get to ten or so that would probably be enough.'

Now in the sort of matches where I play most of my cricket that sort of request is by no means unusual. If a fellow needs another ten runs to get his hundred for the season or if it is a chap's birthday and he has not scored a run all year then there will often be a quiet word in the dressing room beforehand. The aim of the game is after all, to give everyone some fun and a little pleasure.

So we were not too surprised.

Our captain asked him what the occasion was.

'Well, it isn't actually a special occasion,' said the home captain with some slight embarrassment. We try and give him a few runs every week.'

There was a murmuring of protest from our bowlers.

'That's not on,' protested our captain. 'Can't do that.' I'll swear he almost said 'It's not cricket.' He seemed quite offended by the suggestion.

And then the home captain explained just why he was asking for what sounded like a outrageous favour.

It seemed that the batsman in question had sporting ambitions and aspirations which far outweighed his natural skills. But that, although his abilities with the cricket bat were strictly limited, he had a tremendous flair for making money, and a remarkably generous nature.

'Let him get a few runs,' said the home captain, 'and he'll be so pleased with himself that he'll pay the bar bill for the evening.'

'The whole bar bill?' asked our captain.

Their captain nodded.

'Are you sure ten runs is enough?' asked our fast bowler.

It was a good day's cricket, much enjoyed by everyone. Their number four got his ten runs. And the rest of us had free drinks for the evening.

It is good to know that they have their priorities right up in Manchester.

Sunday 9th September

With the English cricket season more or less over, cricket lovers all over the country will now spend the next few months arguing about the composition of the England touring party for the coming winter.

After the team's disastrous summer I cannot help thinking that perhaps the time has come to revolutionise the selection process. Instead of allowing a small group of ex-professional cricketers to pick our representative side, why do we not introduce a more democratic system?

We could, for example, allow all cricket club members to offer their own suggestions for the touring party, with the MCC then using its computer to sort out the most popular team. To avoid the embarrassment of setting off without a wicket-keeper, voters could be instructed to select, say, six batsmen, two wicket keepers, two all rounders and six bowlers. The computer could then pick the six batsmen who attracted the greatest number of votes, the two wicket keepers who attracted the most votes and so on.

It might not ensure a winning team but it would, at least, allow us all to share in the selection process. And that would inevitably remove some of the frustration inherent in the present system.

Monday 10th September
It occurred to me today that it would be possible to put together a team of young cricketers with good connections; young professionals with relatives who have played the game at the highest level. Here is the team I have selected (there are many more eligible players).

1. R A Smith (Hampshire) brother of Chris Smith
2. I P Butcher (Leicester) brother of A R Butcher
3. G S Cowdrey (Kent) son of Colin Cowdrey
4. J P Steel (Glamorgan) brother of D S Steel
5. I A Gregg (Sussex) brother of Tony Gregg|
6. D B D'Oliveira (Worcs) son of Basil D'Oliveira
7. R J Parks (Hampshire) son of Jim Parks
8. A J Stewart (Surrey) son of M J Stewart
9. J D Carr (Middlesex) son of J D Carr
10. D A Graveney (Glos) son of J K Graveney
11. S J Dennis (Yorkshire) nephew of Sir Len Hutton
12. T M Hemlett (Hampshire) son of M E Hemlett

Incidentally, while sorting out that team I started looking at brothers currently playing first class cricket. I found five sets of brothers around the counties: K D Smith and P A Smith (both of Warwickshire), R A Smith and C I Smith (both of Hampshire), J F Steele of Leicestershire and D S Steele of Northants, A P Wells and C M Wells (both of Sussex), and I P Butcher of Leicestershire whose brother A R Butcher plays for Surrey. There may well be more.

Tuesday 11th September
I could not help feeling desperately sorry for Nottinghamshire today. To lose a one-day final by a few runs must be bad enough but to lose the County Championship by such a small margin must be quite unforgettably awful. However, I do feel that Keith Fletcher deserves the success he has had this season. For several years now he has been the best county captain in England and adding the County Championship to the John Player League title seems to prove that quite conclusively.

As I wrote earlier in the season, I would like to see him captaining England this winter.

Wednesday 12th September
So, this is it. The season is over yet again. There are one or two village matches to watch and I have no doubt that we shall play a few more games in the garden. But for the professionals the season is well and truly finished and we must now wait for England to arrive in India and for the West Indians to arrive in Australia. I shall watch the success of Clive Lloyd's team down in Australia with almost as much interest as I watch David Gower's team in India. It will be some

slight comfort if the West Indians can blackwash the Australians too.

Meanwhile, I have packed away my thermos flask and my drinking mug. And made a note to have another go at mending my binoculars.

*1984 Season
Title Holders*

Britannic Assurance County Championship:
Essex

John Player special League Trophy:
Essex

Benson & Hedges Cup:
Lancashire

National Westminster Cup:
Middlesex

We hope you found this book useful. If so we would be grateful if you would post a favourable review on Amazon.

Dr Vernon Coleman is a qualified doctor and professional author who has written over 100 books; these have sold more than two million hardback and paperback copies in the UK alone. His books have been translated into 25 languages and sold around the world. Many books by Vernon Coleman are available as Kindle books on Amazon. For more details about available books please see his author page on Amazon and for more about Vernon Coleman please visit http://www.vernoncoleman.com/

Printed in Great Britain
by Amazon